LIVING WITH MYSELF

3 95

OTHER BOOKS BY WILLIAM E. HULME

Building a Christian Marriage
Your Pastor's Problems
Dynamics of Sanctification
Youth Considers Sex
Pastoral Care of Families
How to Start Counseling
Counseling and Theology
God, Sex, and Youth
Pastoral Care Comes of Age
Dialogue in Despair
Am I Losing My Faith?

William E. Hulme

LIVING WITH MYSELF

Augsburg Publishing House
Minneapolis,   Minnesota

Living With Myself, by William E. Hulme

1971   First Augsburg Paperback

© 1964 by Prentice-Hall, Inc., Englewood Cliffs, N.J.

Library of Congress Catalog Card No. 64-10164

International Standard Book No. 0-8066-1129-4

Manufactured in the United States of America

to Lucy

CONTENTS

PREFACE

This book deals with the problems we human beings experience in living with ourselves — problems that come largely from the estrangement we experience from ourselves and from others. Out of this estrangement come those destructive powers of guilt, anxiety, resentment, and despair that give evidence of our inner division. My purpose is to explore the rationalizations and defenses that we utilize to enable us to live with the illusions that prevent us from coming to grips with this division. Christianity is Good News for the estranged. Its way of reconciliation provides a basis for relating to ourselves and others.

The Christian experience is not apart from the common life but within it. It is a liberating experience from these inner conflicts that stem from estrangement. Even as Christians, however, we may be lacking in this experience. God is more willing to give than we are able to receive. This book is intended to help the reader to receive *more*.

In hoping that this book will be helpful to those who chafe at their bondage to disturbances that hinder their personal development, I am of course including myself as

well as the reader. Liberation is something we grow into
rather than possess. Together we may face the threatening
aspects of our lives within and without. The Gospel's liberation is not only liberation *from* bondage but liberation
into the world of relationships.

The only limits placed on the Good News for the development of our persons are our own self-limitations. We
project onto God and our fellows our own self-rejection and
frustrate their overtures for relationship. I hope that together
we may succeed in limiting these self-limitations.

What have we that we have not received? To attempt to
acknowledge those who have helped in this endeavor would
be beyond my ability to know. During this period of search-
ing I am most keenly aware of the help that has come from
my life together with my family and with the students
with whom I have worked. For what the Spirit has revealed
through these most meaningful relationships I am deeply
grateful.

WILLIAM E. HULME

LIVING WITH MYSELF

1

WHO AM I?

I recall as a child that whenever anyone challenged us with the demand: "Says who!" we would glare at the challenger and shout defiantly, "Me, myself, and I!" That retort invoked a human form of the Trinity. We believed that there was more to us if we described ourselves this way. That we needed three variants of the pronoun to identify ourselves seemed to imply more than complex grammar—it indicated a complex person.

CURIOSITY AND COMPLEXITY

"Says who?" is a good question. Who am I? How can I know myself if I and myself are the same? When I refer to myself as an object, subjects and objects get all mixed up. My ideas become even more complicated when I grow confused about who I am. We have all experienced that moment when we failed to recognize ourselves—when we seemed

1

like a complete stranger to ourselves. A good example of such a moment is the eerie feeling we have when we first hear our own voice played back on a tape recorder. Is that really my voice as others hear it? we wonder.

Of course, the sound vibration from a voice heard within differs from the vibration heard on a tape, and this partially accounts for our inability to recognize our own voices. Yet there is more to it: for whenever we are confronted with an objective view of ourselves, we have the same amazed reaction. I experienced such a reaction when a former teacher of mine recounted an incident which he said had happened when I was a student. As he described my words and deeds in those earlier years, I could neither recall the events nor believe that I could have behaved in such a manner. I experienced a strange feeling as I saw myself through the eyes of another.

At a party one evening, Thomas Nast, the cartoonist, drew caricatures of all the guests. Each person readily identified the caricatures of other guests, but could not recognize his own. Here he was lost. Still another situation occurred during a student performance in which the students were mimicking the mannerisms of certain of their professors. I happened to be sitting near one of the professors who was "getting the works." The actors were clever and the audience rocked with laughter because their mockery was so true to the original. Then I glanced at the professorial victim. His puzzled smile showed that he wanted to join in the laughter but did not have enough to go on. Turning to his wife he asked, "Who is it?"

Even though we may not recognize ourselves by sight or sound, we still are enormously interested in ourselves. Our ears prick up at the sound of our name; our eyes focus sharply if we see it in print. Politicians know how important it is to recall names. A good memory wins them friends and influences elections. One politician on a campaign tour even arranged to have a party member from each town on his itinerary meet him at the preceding railroad stop and familiarize him with the names of the town's important people.

When someone remembers your name it means more than if he just remembered your face. Faces linger in our memories merely because they have been seen before. But when someone recalls your name as well, it seems as if this person is actually interested in you. He remembers me! you think delightedly. A person's name is the key to his identity. In the Bible God's name is used as a synonym for God's nature. Knowing His name is tantamount to knowing Him. Furthermore, when God's attention is directed toward us, He is described as "calling us by name."

As curious as we may be about our own identity, we are unable to find out who we really are. We can look into ourselves, but since we look through our own eyes, this is of little value. Looking into ourselves is like peeling an onion. We remove layer after layer but we never reach the core. Trying to identify ourselves by introspection is like trying to identify a mosaic by getting close to it. The closer we get the more fragmentary and restricted the picture becomes. Whenever a person attempts to know himself without the help of other people, he is likely to encounter a similar loss of perspective.

KNOWING ONESELF BY KNOWING OTHERS

We can know ourselves only in terms of knowing others. In fact it is by knowing others that we develop into persons. Our genes and chromosomes need the stimulation of environment to produce their effects, and our personal relationships form this developmental environment. When a child is born, the parents' task is far from complete—in fact, it has just begun. The kind of relationship we establish with our children contributes as much, if not more, to their development than do the genes we transmit to them. For this reason the parents of adopted children are in many ways the real parents of such children. Through their relationship with each other and with him, the child develops his own identity.

If it is through our significant relationships that we develop into persons, it is also through these relationships that we learn to know who we are—that we develop what we call our self-image. Here we notice a striking difference between delinquent and nondelinquent children. In contrast to the nondelinquent child, the delinquent usually has no clear self-image. He is thoroughly confused about his identity, and much of his problem behavior results from his desperate attempt to establish his identity. In contrast to the nondelinquent child, the delinquent normally has no one whom he admires close by. His heroes are movie actors or television prize fighters—people he has never met. He has little respect for himself or his worth, and the few goals he does have, are unrealistic. Because he does not know himself, he does not know what he either can or wants to do.

Lacking the stimulation of good relationships, the delinquent has not developed personality or character. Like Esau in the Old Testament, he demands immediate satisfactions. He cannot be bothered with any long-range goals since they might necessitate the sacrifice of his immediate desires. The pangs of hunger and the sight and smell of food were enough to make Esau abandon his birthright. He became an easy prey for the cunning wiles of his stronger brother, Jacob who was able to buy Esau's birthright for a mess of pottage! This happened because Esau had too poverty-stricken a spirit to deny a present satisfaction for a future value.

The actions of Peter in the Louis de Rochemont motion picture *Question 7* were quite different. In this story about life behind the iron curtain, Peter also had to choose between an immediate and a future goal. In order to attend the conservatory of music and fulfill his musical ambitions, Peter had to fill out a questionnaire for the Communist state. Question number seven was: "What has been the greatest influence in your life?" Knowing that the only acceptable answer to this question was: "The Communist Party," Peter postponed the decision as long as he could. After he had fled to the West rather than accept a scholarship from the state, his father found the questionnaire still in his room. Peter's answer read: "My father."

Even though we arrive at self-understanding through personal relationships, we have misgivings about what others may think of us. On the one hand, we want to know their opinion—not only because we are curious about how others rate us, but also because we need an objective perspective of our true self. On the other hand, we are really afraid to know what others think of us. They may think less of us than we would hope, and so we may feel more comfortable if we do not know their opinion. Perhaps you have accidentally heard yourself talked about in an uncomplimentary way, or have stumbled upon a report or letter which described you unfavorably. If so, you know what a blow such an experience can be to your self-esteem, and how depressed and panicky you may become over it.

One of the values of group therapy is that each individual has the opportunity to see himself as the others see him. In the intimate association of the group, people become more honest because they develop more insight into themselves

and others. So the stage is set for the realization of the verse
of Bobby Burns:

> Oh wad some power the giftie gie us
> To see oursels as others see us!

Some people, however, consciously or subconsciously block
this opportunity. Then they become disappointed in the
group even though they often realize that it was their own
lack of courage which prevented the group from helping
them. In my own experience with such groups I have discovered a way to overcome this problem. I make each person,
in turn, express his needs to the group and ask for its
help. This method seems to supply the push some need to
overcome their momentary fear. Otherwise their fear might
overcome their deeper desire to know.

GOD OR PEOPLE

When we speak of knowing another we think naturally
of knowing other people. But God, too, can be known. Now
does this knowledge of self come from knowing another
human being or from knowing the Divine Being? Actually,
this is a question we cannot answer. People reveal themselves
to each other only when they feel accepted by each other.
Otherwise they defend and hide themselves. The security
that overcomes fear is the security of being loved. When
we speak of this kind of love we enter the field of religion.
The obligation to love our neighbor as ourselves is coupled
with the obligation to love God with all our hearts.

Actually the obligation to love our neighbor is based upon
the prior obligation to love God. Here is a command which
comes from beyond ourselves. If we are loyal only to self-
imposed standards, then we can change these standards
whenever we wish—we are autocrats. A person can hardly

take himself seriously when he is obligated only to himself. But if our devotion is to the One who is greater than our-selves, we are pulled away from our self-centeredness and its characteristic instability. Since the very nature of self-centeredness is that it cannot encompass love, this obliga-tion to God is of ultimate significance.

That we are created in God's image means that we have a sensitivity to moral values and an ability to think. It also means that we are made for fellowship with God. The story of creation is followed by the story of the fall of man into sin. Yet even in his fall, man lost neither his conscience nor his intelligence. What he lost was his relationship with God.

One of the reasons we say God is personal is because He is identified as love. We do not associate love with things; we associate it with persons. In fact, we associate it with a relationship between persons. Being in God's image is the same as knowing God, for it places us into the most intimate of relationships. But love is never confining; it reaches to others. Nor can it ever be discriminatory since its object is one's neighbor. It is just as impossible to love God and not our neighbor as it is to love this neighbor and not that one.

Because of the inclusive nature of love, knowing oneself, God and one's neighbor are coexisting relationships. Know-ing God provides the necessary humility to love one's neighbor; knowing God cannot exist in isolation. We must have the tangible experience of knowing the love of another person in order to realize the intangible love of God. Further-more, as we grow in self knowledge we also grow in our ability to know God and our neighbor. And—as we have seen—knowing ourselves depends on knowing others.

In the solitude of his Nazi prison cell Dietrich Bonhoeffer realized most clearly how little he could know himself in isolation.

Who am I? They often tell me
I stepped from my cell's confinement
calmly, cheerfully, firmly,
like a Squire from his country-house.

Who am I? They often tell me
I used to speak to my warders
freely and friendly and clearly
as though it were mine to command.

Who am I? They also tell me
I bore the days of misfortune
equably, smilingly, proudly,
like one accustomed to win.

Am I then really that which other men tell of?
Or am I only what I myself know of myself?
Restless and longing and sick, like a bird in a cage,
struggling for breath, as though hands were compressing my
          throat,
yearning for colours, for flowers, for the voices of birds,
Thirsting for words of kindness, for neighbourliness,
Tossing in expectation of great events,
Powerlessly trembling for friends at an infinite distance,
Weary and empty at praying, at thinking, at making,
Faint, and ready to say farewell to it all?

Who am I? This or the Other?
Am I one person today and tomorrow another?
Am I both at once? A hypocrite before others,
and before myself a contemptible woebegone weakling?
Or is something within me still like a beaten army
fleeing in disorder from victory already achieved?

Who am I? They mock me, these lonely questions of mine.
Whoever I am, Thou knowest, O God, I am thine![1]

---

[1] *Prisoner For God* (New York: The Macmillan Company, 1954),
p. 165.

BLOCKAGE IN ONE—BLOCKAGE IN ALL

If knowing self, others and God are bound together, then a blockage in any one of these relationships would cause a blockage in the others. As a minister I come in contact with people who have religious problems—people who complain of a lack of faith, the inability to pray and spiritual deadness. I have learned that little can be gained by confining my attention to the relationship with God. Religious problems are relationship problems, *period.* They are problems not only in knowing God but in *knowing.* More often than not, they are solved by rebuilding in the area of *human* relationships.

Since human fellowship is an integral part of the religious life, this life ceases without such fellowship. Thus it is not a coincidence that the religious life centers in congregations where worshipping God is a corporate act. God apart from people tends to lose a vital part of His meaning. People with religious problems, therefore, are often individuals who have been hurt in their human relationships. Their problem is primarily a matter of the heart and not of the head—a matter of emotion more than one of reason.

Consider the child who has been deprived of the attention and affection of his parents. Perhaps his parents have been preoccupied with work and selfish interests. Or, perhaps they were emotionally deprived in childhood and thus incapable of bestowing a love they themselves had never received. Whatever the cause, how shall the child adjust to this situation? He finds it humiliating to ask for attention and affection only to be ignored or openly pushed aside. He can react in two ways: either he will hate outright those who have denied him love in this manner, or he will seethe with a hate he cannot face because of the guilt it causes him.

In either case his hate may be strong enough to turn him against the adult world. He may seek his identity in the hostile activities of juvenile delinquency, or he may bury his hate within himself and develop neurotic tendencies (which are really only distorted forms of appeals for recognition and affection). By making himself a problem, he continues to demand attention in ways that preserve his self-respect.

The neglected child may, however, give up altogether. Then he simply disciplines himself to do without the affection and concern of close relationships. He continues to have relationships but on an intellectual basis. He builds a rational and defensive wall to imprison his emotions. He has touched the hot stove and has now learned to keep away from it. Although he may not even be aware of his feelings, he has been hurt deeply. He will try to prevent this from happening again.

Suppose the child has chosen this latter way of withdrawal as the solution to his unhappy situation. What will he be like when he reaches maturity? His original childhood situation no longer exists. Despite that fact he continues to live according to the pattern of his childhood because habit patterns which have an emotional basis tend to perpetuate themselves. On the adult level these patterns may be as much of a hindrance to a satisfactory adjustment as they formerly were a help. Thus we find that the child has developed into an adult who still keeps people at a distance. He is affable, witty and concerned about maintaining good public relations even though he sometimes realizes that these result in shallow relationships. Whenever a specific relationship threatens to become emotional, he becomes very uncomfortable. Through long experience he has learned very efficient ways of stifling emotions in himself and in others. Quickly, almost automatically, his tongue goes into action to halt the flow of feelings.

Like most defenses, his also has its cracks. Although he cannot admit it, he too wants affection. He may turn to sex to find it. But when he does, he merely receives the physical expression of sex. The complete, overall relationship sex can represent escapes him. His is a knowing without sharing, and he soon finds out that no marriage can be built upon such an abuse of sex.

There may be times, however, when the crack widens and emotion does break through. The emotion of anger— the emotion of attack is the one most likely to have this effect. Under the stimulus of such an emotion, he definitely relates to another person, but he does so negatively. But even this negative reaction is more genuine and meaningful than his usual superficial relationships. It is not a coincidence that love and hate often go together. Both are evidences of caring. In fact if we love someone, we probably also hate them at times, and if we hate someone with a passion we probably have also wanted his love.

When this anger breaks through, the man is shaken because his defenses are disrupted. He realizes that he really cares, and this is not the picture he has of himself. Emotions are not supposed to have a place in his life, but there they are! Who, then, is he? He realizes now that he does not really know himself at all.

Relationships of knowing—with oneself, with other people and with God—are not relationships we possess or do not possess once and for all. They are relationships that we may have and lose again. In one sense relationships are always in the making. Our immediate task is to look into the problems that we experience when there is a blockage in these relationships.

2
LIVING
WITH MYSELF
ALONE

The students in the seminary where I teach have a year of internship before their last year of study. During this year some serve as student chaplains in institutions where they work with physicians and psychiatrists. On one occasion when I was visiting with a couple who were friends of a student who had recently returned from his internship, the conversation took the following turn: "I don't know—I just don't like to be around Jack as much as I used to," the woman said.

"How come?" I asked.

"Well," she continued, "with all that psychology he had last year I have the feeling he is sitting there analyzing everything I say—looking right through me."

"You don't like that?" I asked.

"No," she answered, "no, I don't."

I was probably feeling sadistic that night for I kept at it. "Something you want to hide?"

At this point her husband chivalrously came to her defense. "After all," he said, "who doesn't have something he wants to hide!"

FEAR OF EXPOSURE

I think we all know what the husband meant. When we isolate ourselves from others—when we live with ourselves alone—we are living with something to hide. This is a natural result of our complex, contradictory nature, for as human beings, we are anything but simple. Our very complexity baffles any attempt to know ourselves.

Often we feel more like two persons than one. We have what the psychologists call ambivalences—that is, we have two opposing wills which demand opposite qualities. Thus, on the one hand we may be weak—and no one knows how weak we can be save our own selves and God. On the other hand we admire the strong even as we despise the weak. We would like to be strong and want others to think of us in this way.

In the matter of feelings toward others we also notice the opposites. We can dislike certain individuals—even to the point of hating them. At the same time we are people who want to be loved, and who would like to think of ourselves as people who love. What makes all this conflict even worse is the unpalatable fact that the people we hate may be the very people we love.

These opposites can continue to plague us in the case of selfishness. Again, nobody knows how completely self-centered and small we can be in moments of irritation or ambition save our own selves and God. But selfishness is not our ideal. In fact we may go to considerable lengths to give others the impression that we are unselfish, for we would like to think of ourselves as selfless.

And, then, we have fears, all kinds of them, and doubts as well—things about us that we would prefer that nobody knew. Yet, we can also be people of faith and again may even surprise ourselves in moments of crisis at the amount of trust in God that we can possess.

All these contradictory tendencies within us lead quite naturally to our showing others only the side that we deem is acceptable to them. Then we live in fear that our other contradictory side will be exposed. We are afraid that we will be proved insincere—a fear that leads us to push down all the harder on that side that condemns us. There is that sudden burst of hatred that we experience toward a loved one. Push it down! There is that unwholesome attitude toward sex. Push it down! There is that disturbing thought that we are a disappointment to those whom we want to respect us. Push it down! There is that jealousy and resentment of people we supposedly like. Push it down! Pushing all this down turns our inner life into a kind of no man's land. Not only do we want others to stay out, but we also reach the point where we cannot bear it ourselves.

The Division Within

Because of this inner conflict over our contradictory nature we develop serious misgivings about ourselves and constantly fear that others will reject us. I remember a cartoon which points this up. It pictured a physician who had just finished examining a patient. Looking at the man rather somberly, the doctor said, "I'm afraid you are allergic—allergic to yourself!" The cartoonist was being more than funny; he was being painfully accurate. We do have an allergic reaction every time we catch a glimpse of what is going on inside of us.

We are afraid of our own shadow, but in this instance the shadow *is* something to be afraid of. The shadow is the term that Fritz Kunkel uses to describe the side opposite the one with which we have identified ourselves. When the sun is not directly overhead we cast a shadow because we are off-centered. So long as we are centered under the sun there is no shadow and we are united in one person. This, according to Kunkel, is our real self because we are at our real center.

When we become off-centered our unity is destroyed. We divide into twins, who are both distortions of the real self. One twin is called the ego or ego-image. He is what we want to be and what we want others to think we are. The other twin is his negative opposite, the shadow, who is out to destroy him. Although we would like to disown the shadow we cannot, for he is as much our self as is our ego-image. Nor can we get rid of him, because the very fact that we have the ego-image means we cast a shadow. Thus he persists in tormenting us with the distasteful knowledge that the self we would like to think we are is not our real self.

Since the shadow is always with us, we live in constant fear that he may rise up at any time and take over. If he did, he would destroy all that the other twin has been trying to build. Therefore, the shadow must be guarded. But he is a cagey fellow. He waits for his moment—the moment when our guard is distracted—to leap forth and openly display the other side of us. The fear that this may happen is really a fear of oneself. For although the shadow's triumph spoils the ego-image, the shadow is really not an *it*. It is an *I,* or rather it *is* I. Of course, this "I" is distorted, but no more so than the ego-image it tries to spoil. The distortions, however, spring from the opposite direction. So long as we are guarded we are not spontaneous. In fact it is in the spontaneous and unguarded moment that the shadow may take control over us. Even though the spontaneous moment is the more genuine moment, it is also the more frightening moment.

Thus, we live in an awesome dread of our own spontaneity, ominously revealing that the division within is as yet only controlled, not healed. It is this spontaneity that the Psalmist fears as he prays, "Keep back thy servant also from presumptuous *sins;* let them not have dominion over me . . ." (Ps. 19:13). The sudden surge of arrogance may get through our guard, and exercising dominion over us, do irreparable harm to our relationships. We are unable to endure the anxiety of being free. Actually it is our use of this freedom that we are unable to endure. For either self may claim it, because unfortunately—or fortunately—we are in both. Therefore, the unpredictable is always a threat and self-sabotage always a possibility.

Soren Kierkegaard, the Danish philosopher, defined dread as the dizziness of freedom.[1] He meant that it is the feeling that comes over a person when he stands at the edge of a precipice and looks into the depths below. He cannot help thinking: What if I should fall? or even, What if I should cast myself into the precipice? To forestall the approaching dizziness he steps back from the edge. This dizziness is partially due to the precipice since it would destroy anyone who fell into it. But the dread is caused also by the eye which looks into the precipice and interprets the sight in terms of possible destruction.

Kierkegaard saw the universality of this dread in the story of Adam. Adam was at peace with himself until the command came from God: "Do not eat of the tree." He became alarmed because this command awakened within him the awareness of freedom. Not only was there a tree with both

---

[1] *Concept of Dread* (Princeton, N.J.: Princeton University Press, 1957), p. 55.

an appeal and a repulsion, there was also a choice. The
command implied that he was able to decide. It is this
fear of "I am able" that constitutes the dizziness of freedom.
For with the possibility of choice, there is also the judgment
upon the consequences.

RUNNING FROM THE JUDGMENT

Although we may go to great lengths to conceal our inner
division, its very existence stamps its mark upon our conscience. This built-in judge pronounces a negative verdict
upon our division and thus nibbles away at our self-respect.
When our mental picture of ourself is lowered this way,
our feelings become even more disturbed. We have pushed
the knowledge of our shadow twin out of our awareness;
nonetheless, anxiety piles up at the edges of this awareness.
No matter how much we try to deceive ourselves, we never
completely succeed, and while this keeps us miserable, it
also keeps us redeemable.

Perhaps we cannot push the shadow completely beyond
our awareness because we are not only the deceived, but
also the deceiver. Here again we see how being both subject
and object complicates our knowing ourselves. It also prevents us from being completely in the dark about ourselves.
I, as object, have difficulty in remaining ignorant of the
fact that I am being deceived by myself, as subject. It is
difficult to keep the left hand from knowing what the right
hand is doing. Charles Lamb revealed the subtleties of this
awareness when he said, "The greatest pleasure I know
is to do a good action by stealth, and to have it found out
by accident."[2]

Even when our attempts to conceal evidence of our

---

[2] *Quoted in* H. E. Fosdick, *On Being a Real Person* (New York:
Harper and Row, Publishers, 1943), p. 98.

shadow are successful insofar as definite incidents are concerned, the feelings which accompanied these incidents remain. These discomforting feelings are now detached from any source, and we must locate some relatively safe situation with which to associate them. Thus, the original situation becomes too painful to retain in our awareness; the mystery of negative feelings without an object is no better; but the reassociation of these feelings with some less threatening situation makes us feel somewhat more comfortable. Unfortunately, the real solution to the problem of living with ourselves has become more remote: instead of being one step from the awareness of our shadow, we are now two steps.

Actually the real solution has not been hindered by this substitution for the safer situation makes it easier for us to seek help. It is something we can talk about without too much pain or embarrassment. What we do not realize, however, is that when we discuss our problems with a counselor, the inner division from which we are running will frequently come to the fore. It must, if we are going to find any real answers. However, the company of another person usually helps us endure the appearance of our less appealing self. Nonetheless, the presence of the negative twin, or shadow, is still a shock—and this is a tribute to the good job we had done in keeping it out of sight.

We are led back to the original division, even though we are discussing a substitute situation because the same feelings are associated with both. Once we begin to express these feelings, the wall of separation between the original shadow and the substitute shadow begins to crumble. Of course, much depends upon the counselor's ability to help us, for when the shadow comes into view, our first reaction is fright. We want to run. Since the counselor is with us, we may have the courage to stay. In fact, he may be in the way if we try to run. As we face the shadow we are shaken by a sudden surge of self-loathing.

All this happened to a man in middle life who came to his pastor because of unaccountable attacks of anxiety. This man was a highly respected leader in both the church and the community and he had served several terms as chairman of the Church Council and was the current head of the United Fund Drive. He liked to think of himself as a person who was doing his best for human betterment. As he talked to the pastor, however, he gave furtive indications that he was discovering the egocentric self behind the noble facade. He was becoming painfully aware that his altruistic endeavors were ways for seeking his own glory. To make matters worse, he constantly received praise, even from the pastor, for his fine services—compliments which served only to compound his guilt. At last he realized that he was even exploiting God, for his activities in the Church Council, like the Kiwanis Club, were merely an excuse for the exercise of his egocentric needs. In despair these words came almost involuntarily from his lips: "What kind of a person am I anyhow!"

In *No Exit,* Jean Paul Sartre dramatizes the conflict between the ego-image and the shadow in the character of Garcin. While still on earth Garcin wanted to think of himself as the tough, masculine, heroic type, or as he phrased it: "Each man has an aim in life, a leading motive; that's so isn't it? Well, I didn't give a damn for wealth, or for love. I aimed at being a real man, a tough as they say. I staked everything on the same horse."[3] Meanwhile, Garcin the coward (the negative twin) lurked behind the scenes and spurred him on in the establishment of this ego-image.

---

[3] *No Exit and Three Other Plays* (New York: Vintage Books, 1955), p. 44.

Whenever this shadow threatened to come into consciousness, Garcin distracted himself by having affairs with women. Being unfaithful to his wife did not bother him, but being a coward disturbed him dreadfully.

Garcin's fear of conflict led him to become a pacifist newspaper editor. When war broke out he tried to flee the country and was captured at the border and shot as a deserter. Sartre's drama takes place in a hell which Garcin shares with Estelle, a voluptuous woman, and Inez, a sadistic woman. The difference between his life on earth and his life in hell is that he can no longer distract himself from his shadow. Why had he fled to the border? Why had he faced death miserably? Why had he not simply refused to fight and faced the consequences? He had his reasons but they no longer seemed valid. He could see his old newspaper office and hear the workers saying, "That chap Garcin was a coward."[4] In six months' time they would be saying, "Cowardly as that skunk Garcin."[5]

His previous method of distraction was still available for Estelle needed escape through love-making as much as he did. But Inez was there to prevent it. Whenever Garcin approached Estelle, Inez would remind him that he was a coward. As long as her eyes were upon him, there could be no distraction. Without any distraction, there remained only the constant and torturous fear that despite all of his heroic dreams, he was finally a coward. Garcin was truly in hell! "Will night never come" he asks?[6] Night *cannot* come for in Sartre's hell the lights are never turned off, and the eyelids can never close.

---

[4] *Ibid.* p. 4.
[5] *Ibid.* p. 4.
[6] *Ibid.* p. 46.

LIMITATIONS OF DISTRACTIONS

While distractions do help in *this* life, the time may come when they no longer satisfy even here. Then the debate between the ego-image and the shadow must begin again. As Sartre has pointed out, this is a debate that cannot be resolved. Even hell does not end it. "Everything's left in suspense forever," because neither the ego-image nor the shadow has the truth. Each is a distortion of a half truth— a corrective to the extremism of the other. Neither contains the self, and while it might seem that the self contains them both, actually it contains neither. For when both ego and shadow are brought into consciousness, they destroy each other. It is then that the real self can emerge. Accompanied by the pains of labor and travail this emergence has all the characteristics of a new birth.

Normally we are not aware that the debate between the ego and the shadow has resumed when distractions cease to satisfy. This is because we have pushed this conflict out of our awareness. Only the feelings connected with the debate return. But what causes the feelings? We experience an apparently genuine confusion over our inner agitation, discontent and tension. The anxiety that has always been lurking at the edges, has moved in. The shadow is coming, or threatening to come into view. Our only defense against this ominous approach of doom is to plunge desperately into new and more stimulating distractions. Like stronger doses of morphine, however, these distractions are ominously temporary. The day arrives when even the most stimulating distraction loses its anaesthetizing power and nothing remains to dull the pain. In the meantime, let us take a look at the defenses and escapes that distract us for awhile.

3
DEFENSE
AND
ESCAPE

Each time my psychology of religion class studied worship the students were skeptical about its value. "Those people in Church," they said, "they're not thinking about what they're saying or singing. They're just moving their lips while their minds are miles away."

"How do you know?" I asked.

"We just know!" they answered.

"That's no answer in a scientific age," I said. "Why don't you find out?"

"How?" they asked.

"Get up a questionnaire," I suggested.

There were six volunteers for the project. Our questionnaire began with questions like: "Why did you come to Church this morning?" The multiple choice answers were: *a.* I wanted to worship God, *b.* Someone in the family wanted me to come, *c.* It's a habit, *d.* It's the thing to do, and so forth. Another question was: "Why did you sing the hymns?" The answers: *a.* I wanted to praise God, *b*. I like to sing, *c*. I didn't sing, and so on. Toward the end we slipped in some sneaky ones. Thus: "Do you remember the content of the Gospel lesson read today?" *a*. Yes, *b*. No. "Do you remember the content of the Epistle lesson read today?" *a*. Yes, *b*. No.

We submitted this questionnaire to some 40 congregations—small, large, rural, urban—immediately after the worship service. The people could quickly and anonymously check the desired answers. The results were most interesting. Of all the people polled, 95 percent came to Church because they wanted to worship God; 96 percent sang the hymns because they wanted to praise God. Obviously we are doing fine! But now we come to those sneaky questions about the content of the Gospel lesson and the Epistle lesson. We can almost see the questionee's pencil heading toward "yes," and hear him say, "But wait! What was that lesson about? I guess the answer is 'no,' but this wouldn't look good, so I'll just skip to the next question." The amazing fact is that one out of four people left the Gospel question blank. One out of *three* left the question concerning the Epistle lesson blank. Yet almost all of them answered the first two questions mentioned.

KEEPING THE CONFLICT OUT OF SIGHT

Thus we bypass the unacceptable. We play little tricks on ourselves—we skip to the next question—to keep the inner division out of sight. There are a host of contemporary defenses and escapes which we use to mask the division within. The most common is busyness. Is there anybody—with the exception of the retired or the unemployed—who is not busy? Busyness is a mark of importance. If a person is not busy, it appears that he has been left out. And who wants to be left out? While ours seems to be the busiest of all cultures, things were not much different in the past. Over a hundred years ago Kierkegaard complained:

> Of all ridiculous things, it seems to me the most ridiculous is to be a busy man of affairs, prompt to meals, and prompt to work. Hence when I see a fly settle down in a crucial moment on the nose of a businessman, or see him bespattered by a carriage which passes by him in even greater haste, or a drawbridge opens before him or a tile from the roof falls down and strikes him dead, then I laugh heartily. And who could help laughing? What do they accomplish, these hustlers? Are they not like the housewife, when her house was on fire, who in her excitement saved the fire-tongs? What more do they save from the great fire of life?[1]

Besides being a badge of importance, busyness is a sop to the conscience. Freedom can be a terrible thing. If I am free then I am accountable. But if I am not free—if I am too busy—then I can escape judgment. This defense extends even to busyness over spiritual matters. In fact the more spiritual the busyness is, the more justifiable it becomes to the conscience. As much as we may chafe under the bondage of busyness, we seem to prefer it to the anxiety and guilt created by freedom. How easily we assume our limitations. "I can't!" or "It's not possible!" or "I have all I can do!" we protest. Then someone else comes along who though burdened by the very same limitations, does the things we say cannot be done! We find it hard to like somebody who destroys our illusions—who pushes our face into the unpleasant reality of freedom.

---

[1] *Either-Or*, Volume I (Princeton, N.J.: Princeton University Press, 1944), pp. 19-20.

Busyness has the additional merit of distracting our attention from inner conflicts. I once attended an educators' conference which became quite worked up over heavy teaching loads. A resolution was put forth requesting college administrations to reduce teachers' hours. In the midst of much enthusiasm for the resolution a venerable educator arose to protest. "Do you know what you are doing?" he asked. "If your hours are reduced, you won't be so busy. Think of all the things you have told yourself you should be doing, but are too busy to do. You won't have any reason now not to do them. Isn't it frightening? We will all be driven to nervous breakdowns. Let us keep our busyness so that we can keep our sanity."

In the midst of your busyness I am sure you have longed to have nothing to do. But what happens when you have nothing to do? How long is it before the pressure starts from within and you load up once more? When we are without anything to do, the conflict which had been projected into the pressure of busyness returns to its source. The temporary integration achieved in fighting the outside pressure is lost as we turn inward to fight ourselves.

Young people have their own peculiar escapes such as running around, goofing off, dashing about, or driving a hot rod a hundred miles an hour down the highway—thus keeping one step ahead of the uprush of disturbance from within. Theirs is a feverish association with a fast crowd made up of other people who are also running away from themselves.

Another escape is alcohol. Although more touted than other escapes, it functions similarly as a distraction by dulling our sensitivity to what is disturbing. In this way alcohol creates an artificial freedom from inhibitions. It also reduces our ability to control ourselves. And thus may lead to a greater problem—alcoholism. Today there are more than seven million alcoholics in America. An even greater problem is the increase of drug addiction with its escape mechanisms similar to those of alcohol.

Like other more socially accepted escapes, alcohol helps a person to live with his pipe dreams. In Eugene O'Neill's *The Iceman Cometh,* a group of bar flies awaited the arrival of a salesman who joined them once a year on his birthday. Each had become dependent upon alcohol to believe in his pipe dream. One was a Harvard graduate who intended to begin a law practice; another was a broken-down politician who planned to reestablish his supremacy in his ward; another was a gambler who was going to open a casino; another a has-been newspaper reporter who intended to resume his post as a foreign correspondent. The salesman's pipe dream was that he loved his wife. Actually he hated her but could not admit it because of her apparent kindliness.

Although the salesman set the drinks up as usual, he did not drink himself. Bothered by his abstinence the others demanded to know what had come over him. The salesman explained that he no longer needed to drink and, furthermore, neither did they. Relentlessly he needled each one of them to start in fulfilling his pipe dream. He did manage to get them out of the saloon, but that was as far as they went. One by one they returned to the bar more desperately in need of alcohol than ever. Cursing the salesman for exposing their self-deception, they drank for the sole purpose of passing out. The police then arrived to arrest the salesman for slaying his wife. It became ironically clear that he no longer needed drink to down his hate because the object of this secret hate was dead. Yet even as he was dragged off to prison the salesman insisted that he had been insane when he said he hated his wife. Seeing a support in this for their own pipe dreams, his comrades gladly believed him.

Whatever we try to push out of our awareness returns

in a disguise. Nothing is ever lost; it simply changes into something else. In the pre-scientific age we thought that to burn was to annihilate. Now we know that burning something simply changes it into something else: solids are changed into gases or even converted into energy. So these repressed conflicts do not disappear. They, too, change into something else.

One of the most common of these transformations is what Dr. Monroe Schindler calls *e.i.i.*—emotionally induced illness.[2] Dr. Schindler estimates that 40 percent of a physician's patients have an emotional cause for their illness. It is easier in our society to talk about a backache than it is to talk about a guilty conscience. If the repressed conflict expresses itself through a physical complaint, it still receives an indirect kind of attention. Often the complaint is labeled *nerves,* and by this compromise permits the symptoms to retain their emotional character while their cause is assigned to something physical. But this face-saving label is an illusion since the nerves, as such, have nothing wrong with them. Furthermore, the real source of the difficulty remains untreated because it is disguised. Thus the last state is worse than the first.

The parable Jesus told about the casting out of devils (Luke 11:24-26), illustrates what we have been saying. He described what happened when an unclean spirit went out of a man. For a time the spirit wandered about the desert seeking a place to dwell. Finding none, it went back to its former home which was now empty, swept and tidy. Then it returned to the desert to seek seven other spirits more wicked than itself, and together they entered the man and dwelt there. In the end the man's state was worse than before!

---

[2] *How to Live 365 Days a Year* (Englewood Cliffs, N. J.: Prentice-Hall, Inc., 1954).

Like that man, we also have very ineffective ways of ridding
ourselves of evil. We either deny its existence, rationalize
it, minimize it or even excuse it. But the house thus cleansed
is open prey for something worse; the evil that we do not
confront directly becomes sevenfold in its intensity. The
judgment that we avoid returns in disguise. And the last
state is worse than the first because now we are dealing with
disguises.

What we refuse to recognize in our alert state may return
to plague us when our guard is down. Fortunately, our
dream life is not as controlled as our waking life. In the
chaotic symbols of dream imagery and in the panic of the
nightmare, the censored conflict finds expression. I have
counseled people whose only awareness of distress was the
recurrence of nightmares. Although they consciously were
unable to see any connection between the nightmares and
their waking life, they lived in constant fear of each approaching evening.

I recall a woman who was on the verge of a nervous
breakdown because of her fear of dreams. Although the
imagery varied, her dream was usually a nightmare in which
she was pursued by someone who was trying to kill her.
The dream was so real that she would suddenly awaken
in a state of utter panic. As far as she was concerned her
life outside of these nightmares was perfectly serene. Obviously the anxiety was rooted in something she had pushed
out of her mind, and the dreams were its disguised expression. This 'something' else turned out to be an affair she
had had with a married man several years before. The clue
came when she mentioned that her dream pursuer was a
woman—evidently a dream symbol of the man's wife. When
she began to talk about this affair, she stammered and
stuttered for the anxiety of the dreams had been trans-
formed into the anxiety of the waking moment. The old

guilt had never been resolved so it disguised itself, demanding attention in the only way she could tolerate. It was only when the disguise itself became unbearable that the woman was forced to come to terms with her problem.

This sort of repressed conflict can cause us to make mistakes or blunders. Fritz Kunkel tells a story about a burglar who had qualms of conscience over being a burglar. Burglary, however, was the only profession the man knew and since he had a family to support, he pushed his misgivings aside and continued to burglarize. Then on one of his jobs he fell down a ladder and broke his leg. In the hospital the combined ministry of psychiatrist, physician and chaplain brought his conflict to light. Though he had pushed his misgivings aside, they had continued to operate subconsciously thus contributing to his fall. In this way he was able to satisfy both sides of his conflict: he decided not to quit his profession; yet he was forced to quit by circumstances which he, himself, had indirectly created.

Like Kunkel's burglar, we also can forget the things we don't want to remember; make mistakes in areas which we are afraid to enter; have accidents in activities over which we have apprehensions about pursuing. We can become confused when clear thinking is painful—go mentally blank when the facts are too threatening to face. If the conflict is severe a complete blackout may be necessary to escape the torturous confrontation.

Going Through the Motions

It is possible to go through the motions of facing our conflicts without actually doing so. There are reasons, other than the desire to come to terms with ourselves, for seeking help. Some people seek help in order to exploit the counselor.

A young lady who had been rejected by her sweetheart is a good example of this type of behavior. She came to her pastor with the problem that she felt guilty over the degree of intimacy that had characterized her broken romance. Naturally the pastor tried to deal with the problem at this level.

He soon discovered, however, that she had another angle. "I'd feel better about this whole thing," she said, "if I knew *he* felt better. Could you arrange a meeting between us?"

What was he to do? He did not want to involve himself. Yet she had asked so pleadingly that he did arrange the meeting.

"Was it satisfying?" he asked when he saw her again.

"Well, yes and no. I think I would feel better if we could get together just once more," she explained.

By this time the pastor realized that what the young lady really wanted was not peace over the past, but her boy friend back. Everything else was a cover-up for this. She was attempting to use the pastor as go-between or fixer.

Some people seek help only because they want relief from pain. They have to *talk* to somebody. After they have talked their problem out they feel relieved. But talking a problem out is only the first step in self-confrontation. The next step involves making some necessary changes in one's life. Yet for some the first step is sufficient. They are satisfied with temporary relief and do not return for help until the pressures again build up.

Then there are people who seek help to show they are trying—to show they are sincere in their desire to overcome their problems. Once they have obtained help the fact that they are not trying becomes easier to bear. What they have really done is transfer the problem to someone else. Since they are not serious, the counseling itself becomes an escape from responsible action.

We find this situation in any age which like ours emphasizes counseling. In the court of Louis XIV of France, for example, counseling was the rage. It became the fashion for each of the nobility to have a spiritual director. Many of these people were simply bored with court life and were dabbling in introspection and spiritual exercises for diversion. The results were cynically exposed by a writer of this period. "What sort is the lady who has a director?" he asked. "Is she kinder to her husband and gentler to her servants? Is she one with a less execrable temper, and a less relish for the comforts of life? No, not a bit of it. What then, is she? Just a lady who has a director."[3]

This same kind of exploitation may exist in our religious pursuits. We can avoid God not only by shunning religion, but also by being involved in religious activities. It is easier to deceive ourselves when we are going through the motions than when we are avoiding the motions. The more honest way of avoiding God's Word, according to Kierkegaard, is to toss it aside—to refuse to be alone with it. But there is another way of defending ourselves against God's Word and that is "in sheer defiance dare to be alone with it (yet not actually alone). Take the Holy Scriptures, shut your door—but then take ten dictionaries and 25 commentaries —then you can read it just as quietly and coolly as you read the newspaper."[4] This same danger is inherent in the use of religious rituals as a whole. Religious techniques for the release of guilt, which avoid the emotional dimensions of this guilt, are more likely to repress it than to release it. This repressed guilt is kept in check by a variety of religious

---

[3] K. D. Little, *Francois De Fenelon* (New York: Harper and Row, Publishers, 1951), p. 35.
[4] *For Self Examination* (Minneapolis: Augsburg Publishing Co., 1940), p. 33.

activities which constitute a continuous means of atonement and create a compensatory holier-than-thou attitude.

A similar misuse of effort is prevalent in the field of
psychology. Psychology has been used to escape from conflicts as well as to resolve them. As an academic discipline,
psychology is a convenient defense for those who would
rather intellectualize than solve their problems. It is always
easier to fight the battle when we use intellectual concepts
than when we deal directly with our disturbed feelings.
Confining the battle to an intellectual front is a retreat from
the "blood and guts" of total encounter.

DEFENSE BASED ON FEAR

All of these defenses and escapes are motivated by fear.
Lewis J. Sherrill said, "The human organism seems capable
of enduring anything in the universe except a clear, complete, fully conscious view of one's self as he actually is."[5]
Obviously this uncensored view of the self is unendurable
because it creates a terrible fear. It is fear first of all of
judgment. After such a view the involuntary response is
like that of the prophet Isaiah's: "Woe is me for I am undone!" We are frightened by the contrast between what we
are and what we feel obligated to be. This is the judgment
of conscience which as Shakespeare said, "makes cowards of
us all."

But this fear is also a fear of change. It takes a certain
amount of security to be able to tolerate improvement. Like
the rest of creation, human beings are also governed by the
laws of inertia. A body set in motion is hard to stop and a

---

[5] *Guilt and Redemption* (Richmond, Va.: John Knox Press, 1945),
p. 90.

body that is stopped is hard to start. We have our own brand
of checks and balances with which we maintain the status
quo. We learn to make some sort of an adjustment to the
way things are, and any threat to this adjustment causes
us serious emotional repercussions. At the heart of our adjustment is our self-image. The checks and balances that
preserve the status quo are also protecting our self-image.
Any need for improvement is in effect a judgment upon our
self-image.

We have a need to defend the past because we have
helped to create this past. What we are trying to avoid is
the fact that the adjustment we have made may be open to
question. When somebody rocks the boat we become irritated. It is annoying to know that we have the potential
for doing things differently. The very thought throws us
afresh into the anxiety of freedom from which our adjustment was protecting us. Even when our lot is miserable
there is comfort in knowing that there is nothing we can
do about it. In this way we escape the greater misery of
judgment.

People who come to a counselor are often very discouraged. One would think they desired help to change
their situation. Consciously they do. But often they are
more under the control of subconscious forces which want
to preserve the status quo. They seem to desire to demonstrate to the counselor that either they or their situation
is unhelpable—unredeemable. There is more comfort in
being the victim of unpleasant circumstances than in being
the creator of these circumstances. The very fact that
something can be done is a judgment on the person for not
having done it. No wonder he can fail to comprehend or
even to hear any such suggestion.

What we have been describing is the age-old resistance to
repentance. Repentance is the act of a free man. His sorrow

is not that he could do no other, but that he could have done otherwise. It is a sorrow over the misuse of his freedom. But repentance is not only sorrow. It is sorrow with hope. The past can be judged because there is hope for the future. Repentance is the means by which the inertia of inadequate adjustments can be overcome. It is the change in the self-image brought about by the crisis of judgment.

4
PROTECTION FROM PEOPLE

⊕

In the last chapter we discussed the escapes and defenses we use to avoid any direct confrontation with our inner conflicts. These same conflicts also cause trouble in our relationships with others. For if we cannot bear to see ourselves as we are, we surely do not want others to perceive the truth about us. If we will go to such lengths to distract our own attention from our inner conflicts, imagine how far we will go to protect ourselves from exposure to others! I remember that as a child I hid behind the door when the music teacher arrived to give me my first piano lesson. Although I knew that this was no permanent solution to my problem, I was at least postponing the day of reckoning.

The tendency to hide has been our first line of defense since Adam tried to hide from God in the Garden of Eden. Regardless of how temporary the security we achieve is, we are comforted by the fact that at least for now we are unexposed. Actually we are indulging in a childish game of hide and seek: we are secure only if we stay out of sight; but if we stay hidden we will not be able to reach the goal. Fear has a way of giving priority to the present tense.

Basically, there are three ways we use to try to protect ourselves from exposure.[1] These are: withdrawal from others; servile attachment to others; and attack on others. Each of these ways offers a person temporary security for a stiff price: he forfeits the possibility of genuine relationship with others. Each of these methods also helps to preserve the emotional isolation that characterizes individuals in our culture. Although each way differs radically in approach from the others, they are all characterized by a profound distrust of human nature. They are based upon the axiom: others will hurt me if they can; therefore, I must not allow myself to become vulnerable.

Withdrawal

The way of withdrawal consists in putting a safe distance between ourselves and others. The strategy is that if I do not get close to you, you cannot see me, and if you cannot see me, you cannot hurt me. The withdrawal may be a geographical one in which we avoid being in another person's line of vision. When contact threatens to become unavoidable we surreptitiously cross to the other side of the street.

The person who withdraws is often shy—he fears being rejected by others. Since he finds his security in making himself inconspicuous, overtures to draw him out only

---

[1] I am indebted for this division to the book by Karen Horney, *The Neurotic Personality of Our Time* (New York: W. W. Norton & Co., Inc., 1937).

frighten him into further withdrawal. He is a "loner" who finds his own company safe and therefore preferable.

The withdrawal may be psychological rather than geographical. It is possible to be surrounded by people and yet remain hidden. The withdrawing person can erect a wall around himself so that people think they know him but in reality do not. This psychological wall permits him to see into others but prevents them from seeing into him. Thus he can safely make contact with others without becoming involved with them. There is no sharing and no participation, however, only observation. If the wall were to be pulled down, the withdrawing person would experience the same panic that a shy person does when he is forced into conspicuous contact.

Few of us consciously withdraw as a protection from people. Rather we do so unconsciously by rationalizing our actions in order to make our withdrawal excusable. Instead of calling our emotion fear, we justify it as indifference. "I don't want to" sounds better than "I'm afraid to." Also "I don't want to" ends the matter, while "I'm afraid to" carries with it the pressure of change. Fear is not an acceptable motivation. We feel ashamed if we have to admit it. On the other hand, "I couldn't care less" creates an impression of superiority.

In group sessions where individuals are sharing with each other, one or two may remain aloof. Although they may comment or even give advice to those who do share, they never share anything of themselves. When pressed by the group to truly participate, their usual defense is to say that they have no need to share, or that they have no desire to share with this particular group. The necessity of having to defend their withdrawal, tends to reinforce it. At best this creates the impression that they are superiorly self-sufficient; at worst that they are smugly looking down upon the others.

Those who withdraw geographically may defend themselves in the same smug way. They say that they prefer plants, animals or even things to people; what they mean is that plants, animals or things are not as threatening as people. Unlike human beings, these things cannot talk back, judge, or reject them, and therefore they are more at ease apart from others. Thus, an "I-couldn't-care-less" attitude is actually a defense against caring—the battle for acceptance looms too big or too long and indifference seems to offer the only safe route to self-respect. This happens precisely because the individual cares so much!

The need for intimacy with others is with us from the beginning. Harry Stack Sullivan says that an infant perceives when its mother feeds it with tenderness and may reject her nipple when she withholds this tenderness even though it may be hungry. Tenderness at this interpersonal level is necessary for the satisfaction of *all* of the infant's needs. When this tenderness is not forthcoming, the infant cries. If by crying the infant does not succeed in securing the tenderness it craves, it may become apathetic on what appears to be a secondary, although dangerous level of adjustment. This apathy is a sign of the infant's desperate need; not of its lack of need.[2]

In the same way a maturing adult may detach himself emotionally from others in an effort to compensate for their lack of acceptance. He resists involvement with others for fear of exposing himself to further hurt. He walls in his shaky confidence with an air of aloofness, hiding his need for others behind a facade of self-sufficiency. But his adjustment is at the lower level of a truncated existence.

---

[2] *The Inter-personal Theory of Psychiatry* (New York: W. W. Norton & Company, Inc., 1953), pp. 55-57.

SERVILE ATTACHMENT

The way of servile attachment is based upon the idea that if I make myself congenial and indispensable, you will be tolerant of me even if you recognize me for what I am. Here the individual concentrates on making friendly and helpful overtures to others instead of ignoring them. But his overtures are as calculated as those of the shrewd steward in the Biblical parable. (Luke 16: 1-13) This steward had been accused of wasting his master's goods and was faced with dismissal. He had to protect himself against this frightening prospect and so he decided to ingratiate himself with certain people. Then, when his shame became known, they would still feel obligated to him. So he called in his employer's debtors one by one and reduced the amount of their debt. Naturally they were grateful to him. Even his employer had to marvel at his ingenuity. When his day of reckoning came, he had "friends" to take him in.

In a similar way those who attach themselves servilely to others are depending upon their strategy to protect them when all else fails. They try to be helpful and agreeable. But behind this kindly facade is a frightened individual who has serious misgivings about his own worth. His apparent congeniality and generosity has its price, for he is buying protection. But it also extorts a price from him: in trying to please he sacrifices his individuality. Motivated by fear, his actions become predictable and finally monotonous. In the most simple and obvious way he is the other-directed person whom David Riesman describes.[3] Riesman believes that our culture is characterized by people who allow themselves to

---

[3] *The Lonely Crowd* (New York: Doubleday & Company, Inc., 1953).

be governed by what others think. They are the victims of a conformist society which can tolerate at the most only a few deviates.

Yet this same society despises its own victims. People do not respect the weakness in others which they are exploiting at the same time. At a convention of young people I once witnessed a pathetic example of this kind of exploitation. One of the teen-age girls who had problems in relating to her group did the washing for six other girls so that they would tolerate her in their company. Obviously they took advantage of her for all she was worth.

A person who effaces himself to please others is known as a "nice guy." He is also regarded as a "lightweight." Because he offers no threat, there is no reason to attack him, but there is also no reason to rate him with importance for he is easily taken for granted and his sensitivities can be ignored. Yet no one is without individuality, not even the servile person. He may hide his individuality behind a disarming smile which he continues to wear even when he is relating bad news. In counseling with such an individual the counselor knows that so long as the conversation is accompanied by the smile, the real person is not coming through. But there are those moments when the real person does break through—when the hidden facts unexpectedly emerge into the open. These are heavy, even depressing moments, but they are honest moments. It is then that the smile departs, for it is no longer needed.

Although this servile congeniality originated as a protective device, it can become so habitual that it functions almost automatically. As a college sophomore I recall leading a group of blindfolded freshmen to the girls' dormitory to pray for rain while the girls doused them with water from the windows above. One of the freshmen wandered out of line, and before anybody could stop him, he walked straight into a tree. He swayed a bit from the blow, then bowed slightly in the direction of the tree and said, "Pardon me."

The need to please is greatest in a face to face encounter. Have you noticed how much more polite people are when they are on foot than when they are driving an automobile? The automobile seems to provide all the protection from people they need and so they can more safely expose their aggressive tendencies. Similarly, people will speak more boldly to each other in a group situation than when they are alone with each other. For when there are only two people present, they have a compulsive fear of rupturing the rapport, and protect themselves by being congenial. They are incapable of any overtures that would create conflict. Thus their friendliness stops short of helping the other to face any unpleasant truth. It is much easier for them to apologize than to criticize. Emotionally they are more predisposed to guilt than to anger.

ATTACK

The way of attack is preventative warfare. The idea is to go after others before they come after you. The aggressive nature of this protective device seems to belie the fact that it is motivated by fear, but we rarely realize that it is caused by fear. The juvenile delinquent is an example in point. He gives every indication of being fearless as he defies authority; but his very hostility is an outlet for his concealed anxiety. His quick resort to attack comes from an instinctive fear of people. For him to protect himself by servile attachment would be the most abhorrent kind of self-surrender. Even people who are servilely congenial may attack when their hidden hostility becomes too much to hold back; when their strategy of servility encounters humiliating failure; or even when there is no possibility that they may be exposed. The polite little boy at the party may surreptitiously pinch and punch when someone mischievously turns off the lights.

People who choose the way of attack believe that the best defense is a good offense. For them life is a meanly competitive business. The only way to keep others from putting you in the doghouse is to put them in first, for if you give people the opportunity, they will take advantage of you. Beneath this uncomplimentary image of others lies the hidden uncomplimentary image of the self. If I am this way then they must be this way also. And if they are—I am in danger. Therefore, the only way to survive in such an arena is by using openly competitive tactics which characterize athletics.

This is basically the point of view of the wrestler. His survival depends upon being on top. Being on top, of course, means being on top of someone else who, of necessity, must be on the bottom. The state of alarm occurs when someone happens to get on top of us. Then we are on the bottom and in imminent danger of being pinned. Our security obviously depends upon not being put into such a vulnerable position, and the only way to do this is to keep the positions reversed. The justification for such reasoning is derived strictly from the assumptions of competitive sports. But since the struggle is for more than the laurels of an athletic victory, the attitude of the competitor is characterized by the rigidity of desperation.

The fact that the assumptions of the sporting arena can be transferred to life as a whole is a good indication of the highly competitive nature of our culture. The attacker can beat others out in legitimate competition. From childhood he has been indoctrinated in a win-or-else cutthroat competitiveness that channels and perhaps even helps to create his paranoid compulsiveness to attack. The mores of this aggressive approach to people are accepted as necessary for the

establishment of personal worth. When personal worth depends upon competitive accomplishment, the way of attack
is obviously the way of self-preservation.

Our employment of the method of attack can also determine the kind of relationship we establish with people. If
we dominate another person, we are in an indirect sense
beating him down. In a group situation we try to "run the
show." In all of his personal associations the attacker has a
compulsive need to be boss. Of course this means he has to
choose his associates carefully, for not all people are weak
enough to tolerate his domination. But since his policy is,
"If I can't have my way, I won't play," the selective process
goes relentlessly on.

Our attack may be direct as well as indirect. We can pick
on people and aggravate them. We can do this openly by
simply bullying people, or (and this is more often the case)
we can subtly make them feel stupid and inadequate. There
are many "innocent" ways in which this can be done. For
example, suppose you know by the grapevine that a certain
person has failed an examination. To aggravate him you
need but "innocently" ask him how he fared. The attack is
all the more effective if there are others within earshot.

The more we know a person the more we know where his
sensitivities lie. This is why brothers and sisters can torment
each other so effectively and why husbands and wives undermine each other's confidence so efficiently. Each has discovered through the privileges of intimacy the whereabouts
of his partner's Achilles' heel. Each knows how to hit the
glass jaw and to pummel the solar plexis. In moments of hostility each abuses his privilege and takes advantage of his
knowledge.

In contrast to the person who is servile, the attacker is
a poor apologizer, for hostility is to the fore rather than
guilt. We counselors are aware that the negative emotion

that is most easily expressed may not be the emotion at the
source of the disturbance. So we look for the opposite. In
guilty people we are alert for hostility and in hostile people
we are alert for guilt. Those who attack give no quarter and
usually ask for none. Consequently, they are the most
difficult group to help.

DAMAGED SELF-IMAGE

We cannot classify people as if they were things. Everyone of us, to some extent, participates in the whole gamut of
human experience, but we usually exhibit some characteristics more than others. If you recognized your own actions
in any of the devices which I described above, I am sure
that this discovery made you unhappy. Although these ways
are designed to protect us, they also contribute to our dam-
aged self-image. When we withdraw, we heighten our
awareness that we have something to hide. When we behave
servilely, we are aware that much of this behavior is a
facade. When we attack, we are aware that we are also
inflicting hurt.

Any contrast between our inner self and our outer self
registers negatively on our conscience—even as it blocks
our relationship with others. Although we may be consciously unaware of our self-centered motivations, they nonetheless take their toll of our self-respect. Because it is difficult
to help others until we have come to grips with ourselves, I
have my beginning students read a book that exposes these
secret maneuvers of the inner life.[4] This is often a shocking
experience. In the students' words: "it hits home." By

---

[4] *Such as* Horney, *op. cit., or* Albert Camus, *The Fall* (New York:
Alfred A. Knopf, Inc., 1961).

"home" they mean that it touched upon a hidden awareness. The book exposed what the student had dimly known.
All of these indictments had registered before, but because
they were negative he had chosen to ignore them. His present shock is due to his inability to keep his secrets from
himself any longer. The bull's eye was hit because it was
magnetized to draw the arrow.

When the students begin their ministry to others I have
them write up their visits in dialogue form. Then I, in turn,
comment upon their reports. On one such report I remarked
that the student seemed to have difficulty in relating in any
depth with others. In spite of my attempts to point out the
other positive aspects of his visit, the student was severely
shaken by this criticism. He said that my criticism had
matched his own undefined awareness of the same thing. His
resistance to defining his weakness was overcome by a pressure from without—namely from my observation. Thus, he
was "hit."

These examples show that we can recognize ourselves in
the mirror if we stand directly in front of it, but we resist
the direct gaze. When we receive an assist from without,
however, we may be unable to avoid really seeing ourselves.
The result is always upsetting, yet it can be the beginning of
a more honest relationship with ourselves. It may also cause
us to turn in anger upon the one who provided the assist.
In fact our first reaction toward the person who holds up the
mirror is usually anger. He is the destroyer of our happy
illusions, and we hate him for this. As one young man confessed to me, "I have been having serious misgivings over
you. Last week you seemed to want me to dislike my mother.
I didn't like you for this." The sad truth was, however, that
he *did* dislike his mother, but his whole world would
crumble if he recognized this fact.

This young man's reaction illustrates, to a certain extent,

the nature of the subconscious. Now let us examine the workings of the subsconscious in greater detail. Suppose there was some object you did not want to see. Let it represent this inner conflict that threatens to destroy you. Suppose that you turn away from this object and convince yourself that it does not exist because you no longer see it. You ignore the fact that you could turn your head to see it. Now let someone come along and inform you that this fearful object is present. You insist emphatically that it is not— that you ought to know since you can see perfectly well. Suppose now he takes the next step and tries to turn your head in the right direction. What would be your immediate reaction? You would probably push him away and heatedly order him to take his hands off you. In a similar way we guard our subconscious. Much of what is in our subconscious we have willed—usually out of fear—to go there. Now it is our will to keep it there. But it is always threatening to come into view; hence our anxiety.

5
HOSTILITY
IN
ACTION

As we have seen, each of the three ways of protecting ourselves from people—withdrawal, servile attachment and attack—indicates a hostile or hateful attitude toward people. This attitude is obvious when we attack; it is less apparent when we withdraw or become servilely attached, but it is present, nonetheless, though in a hidden way. In these instances our hostility manifests itself indirectly. For example, we enjoy hearing the worst about people, even about those with whom we are supposedly on good terms.

"Have you heard about So-and-so?" someone will ask.

"No," we say almost eagerly, "what about him?"

"Well, I don't know whether I should say anything about it," says our informant, but following a short encouraging silence, he furnishes us with the sordid details.

"No!" we say, as though shocked into incredulity by the revelation—"No, not So-and-so! Why, he is the last person I would expect to get himself involved in something like that. Well, I guess you never can tell, can you!"

About a week later we see our informant again and almost as an aside he says, "Oh say, do you remember what I told you about So-and-so?"

"Oh yes," we answer, "is there more?"

"Well, yes, in a way," he says. "I found out there is nothing to it."

"Oh," we say, and for a split second we realize we are disappointed. We recover quickly our equilibrium. "I'm surely glad to hear it." "I never saw how such a thing would be true about him anyhow."

In the old comic strip, "From Nine to Five" the office girls, Hysteria, Wysteria, Calorie, Coma and the others gathered regularly for a coffee break. And they did what we often do in our own gatherings—they talked about the persons who were unfortunate enough not to be present. In one particular incident Jane was "getting it" from the others. Hysteria however had some qualms about participating. "Listen, girls," she said, "Jane is my friend, and I wouldn't say anything against her for the world—but I'm sure willing to listen!"

Most of us have discovered that while it is not difficult to get someone to listen and sympathize with us when we have had a tough break, it is very difficult to get anyone to listen and sympathize when we have had a good break. When corrected examination papers are returned to students —even theological students—each hastily asks the other, "What mark did you get?" The idea is to find out how he did in comparison to the others. There is no honest rejoicing at the good grade of another; there may even be resentment. If the answer is positive, the inquirer feels obligated to say, "Good for you." But what he thinks is "Nuts!" In the same way we force out the words "congratulations" to the happy recipient of an award, a promotion or an exclusive invitation, but, allow the conversation to die out because we're too jealous to enjoy another's good fortune.

How much better things would be if we were honest. Our society, unfortunately, is not ready for honest communication. At any rate, we do not think it is, and therefore bottle up the innumerable irritations and resentments we feel but cannot allow ourselves to express. These repressed emotions demand some form of release, and we wait for that moment when we can acceptably (and indirectly) express our hostility. When the moment is at hand, however, more is likely to pour out than the immediate situation seems to warrant. Thus every safe moment for the expression of hostile feelings also becomes a scapegoat moment.

Not All on the Debit Side

The release of hostility is not always a bad thing. There are times when such a release may be necessary in order for the individual to maintain some sort of vitality. The Stranger in Albert Camus' novel of the same title illustrates this. He was a person who gave no evidence of having a self. He never asserted himself because it was easier to go along with others than to resist them. He did not care enough about anyone to love or hate. He agreed with people in order to be rid of them. While in prison awaiting execution for a senseless crime, he was the "atheist in the foxhole." Because he did not exhibit the fears common to people facing death, he was a source of frustration to the priest who tried to minister to him.

The priest ignored the Stranger's absolute resistance and continued to prod him with questions about God and the life hereafter. Suddenly the Stranger came to life. With an intense fury he began to berate and to pummel the priest. The "counselor" had "gotten through," in a way that he had not anticipated. The Stranger had become an angry person. His fury had "washed him clean" and "emptied him of hope," so that he was able to face death with an anticipation of freedom. All he desired was that people would jeer at him as he went to the guillotine so that he could maintain his newly-discovered self-affirmation.[1]

Since we can hate the person we also love, our intimate relationships can be quite turbulent. Yet, hate like love, is a sign of deep caring. When we are indifferent to another, we ignore him. This is quite different from *trying* to ignore him—for the very effort betrays our deeper feelings. When love is frustrated, it turns into hate before it dies in indifference.

Not all hostility is the underside of love. In our anger we may simply be using a scapegoat. This is particularly true in family relationships. Because they are bound together by many factors, members of a family can accept more hostility from each other than members of other groups normally tolerate. This is a tribute to the security within the family circle which family members often exploit when they take out their frustrations on each other. The home turns into a torture chamber wherein each member torments the other until nobody has any defenses or illusions left. Since these defenses and illusions are actually obstacles to individual growth, their collapse may prove beneficial, and the individual may experience a crisis which will help his development. Unfortunately, this is rarely the outcome of family crises for they usually lead to further frustration.

Eugene O'Neill's description of his own family life in

---

[1] Camus, *The Stranger* (New York: Alfred A. Knopf, Inc., 1946), p. 154.

Long Day's Journey into Night[2] is a frightening illustration of the sterility of family conflict. In this play, the father, mother and two brothers alternated between submission and attack, between hatred and guilt, and between breaking their ties and cementing them. The mother would complain to the sons about the father, and when the sons would support her against him, she would rebuke them for lack of respect.

One minute the youngest son, Edmund, would tell his father, "I hate your guts," and the next minute would dully say, "I didn't mean it, Papa." His affection was something that could only be temporary. Soon he would start to needle his father again, and in a bursting rage would denounce him as a "stinking old miser." Once Edmund summed up the family conversation by saying sardonically, "We don't seem able to avoid unpleasant topics, do we?"

Life for this family was a series of emotional crises that led to nothing. Their family, like far too many such histories, substantiate the ancient Greek interpretation of life as a series of meaningless cycles leading nowhere—a long day's journey into night.

This same sense of going nowhere pervades Samuel Becket's play, *Waiting for Godot*. Despite the cryptic nature of this tragicomedy, there is an obvious tension between the two characters, Estagon and Vladimir. They can neither stand each other or stand to be apart from each other. To Vladimir's accusation that he is a hard man to get on with and that it would be better if they parted, Estagon replies, "You always say that and you always come crawling back."

Vladimir answers, "To every man his little cross. Till he dies. And is forgotten."[3] Even when these two manage to

---

[2] (New Haven: Yale University Press, 1956), p. 137.
[3] (New York: Grove Press), 1954, p. 40.

get along, their life seems meaningless. Thus Estagon asks if it would be a good thing if he tried on his boots and Vladimir answers, "It'd pass the time. I assure you, it'd be an occupation."

"We always find something, eh Didi, to give us the impression we exist?" Estagon answers.[4] Only by maintaining the illusion that they are waiting for Godot—someone or something will change things—can they tolerate the repetition of their meaningless behavior patterns. Like O'Neill's family, they show what Schopenhauer meant when he said, "People like porcupines huddle together for warmth and then draw apart again because of the pricks in the spine."

Misgivings of Hostility

Because hostility is something we are not supposed to have, we have difficulty in dealing with it directly. Our attempts to control our hostility may only stockpile it. When it does come out, we are often shocked by its intensity. The freshman fraternity pledge thinks the sadistic sophomore is an uncomplicated cad. But the sophomore may be having as many misgivings over his behavior as the freshman. As one sophomore put it: "Why is it that I have no intention of overdoing it in the paddle line, but before I realize what I am doing, I am cracking those poor freshmen as if I hated them. I seem to lose my head." Actually this sophomore was exploiting a rare opportunity to express his hostility legitimately. But he had more hostility stored up than he realized, and when it came out, it practically took possession of him.

---

[4] *Ibid.,* p. 45.

The counseling relationship offers an opportunity for this stored-up hostility to be released not only legitimately but also harmlessly. While the counselor is aware of this, he may be taken off guard by the sudden intensity of the release. I recall one hot summer day when I was counseling a man who was unhappily employed. As he haltingly described his intolerable working conditions, he began to associate them with comparable conditions in his family life. Even though I encouraged him to express his feelings concerning these family ties, I was unprepared for the suddenness with which his feelings broke loose. His long-seething sense of outrage seemed to explode as he shouted out his denunciations with an almost hysterical fury.

Completely overcome by the force of his anger, this heretofore reserved man was now oblivious to the fact that the windows were open and that people might hear him. I was torn between the desire to shut the windows and fear that such an interruption would stop him short. I decided to leave the windows open, and later the man himself became concerned over whether he had been overheard. This was a delicate moment—the point where the shock over the intensity of the released hostility could lead to further repression. Many of us seem to have a sixth sense about what might happen if we ever let go with our anger, and the very fear of losing control makes us continue to repress that anger.

Such accumulated hostility begins to corrupt our relationship with God. Here, we might think, is the one area where there is no hostility. What we mean is that it is the one area where there should be no hostility, and it is this very word *should* that causes all the trouble. Paul Tillich penetrates the barrier of the *should* when he asks: "Have you ever noticed how much hostility against God dwells in the depths

of the good and honest people, in those who excel in works
of charity, piety, and religious zeal?"[5] We see this hostility
behind the compulsion to pacify God. Obviously we fear his
rejection, and it is impossible not to feel hostile toward
anyone who rejects us. But this fact is difficult to face,
particularly in relation to God for if we do face it, the only
alternative seems to be despair.

Martin Luther faced a similar predicament before the
Reformation. In the motion picture, *Martin Luther,* the unhappy monk went to his spiritual director, Johan von Staupitz, the vicar of his Augustinian order, and confessed: "I
have committed the unpardonable sin."

Von Staupitz hurriedly motioned the other monks to leave
the room. "Now," he said with anticipation, "what is this
sin?"

"My sin," said Luther, "is that I cannot love God."

The counselor was taken aback. "Why can't you love
God?" he asked.

"Because," answered Luther, "my God is too unlovable
to love."

The stockpile of hostility may never reach an explosive
point. Rather it may reach a stage where it begins to seep
out of its confinement and change our whole attitude toward life, distorting our outlook so that we meet life with
a grievance. A distortion of this nature can lead to paranoid
disturbances, in which the sick person is convinced that
everybody is against him. The mentally ill differ, not in kind
but merely in degree, from those who are well. Paranoid
tendencies exist in all of us at one time or another. When
they become too strong they interfere with our ability to get
along with others.

---

[5] *The New Being* (New York: Charles Scribner's Sons, 1955),
p. 20.

The stockpile of hostility makes us more interested in retaliation than in reconciliation. In our own minds, we are quite sure that we have been abused and we want somebody to pay for our troubles. Unfortunately, much of our resistance to reconciliation is confined to the underground of the subconscious. Had we but the courage perhaps we would appear as adamant as Soren Kierkegaard's personified "clerical error." This "clerical error" was an error made by a writer's slip of the pen that became conscious of its existence as an error. The error refused to allow itself to be corrected and defiantly said to the writer, "No, I will not be erased. I will stand as a witness against thee that thou art a very poor writer."[6] In the same way we may not be willing to let others off—even God—with a simple erasure.

BASIC ANXIETY

Because hostility interferes with our relationship to others, it also interferes with our own security. It cuts us off from others and therefore leaves us feeling alone and helpless in the midst of a hostile world—a predicament which Karen Horney calls the basic anxiety.[7] Our principal need is to believe in the loyalty of others, but our own projected hostility creates distrust of others. I once asked a very effective preacher how he was able to deliver an organized sermon without notes. "I owe it to two principles that I practice," he replied. "One is that I trust my memory rather than doubt it. The other is I assure myself that my hearers are *for* me rather than against me." Because of the awareness of our own hostility it is hard to believe that people are

---

[6] *Sickness unto Death* (New York: Doubleday & Company, Inc., 1954), p. 207.
[7] Horney, *op. cit.*, p. 89.

for us. It is more natural to believe that they are against us. As someone said, "No one begins to climb the ladder very high before his fellows begin to shake it."

When we ourselves have the desire to shake someone else's ladder, we find it natural to suspect that others would like to shake ours. "To the pure all things are pure, but nothing is pure to the tainted (Titus 1:11). We assume that others are just waiting for us to make a slip so that they can laugh at our discomfort. The worst punishment that the ancient Hebrews could imagine was that God would make them the laughingstock of their neighbors, and we fear the same thing. We also fear that even our friends may become enemies. For in our hostile eyes they, too, seem to be out to disprove us, to resist us. In the last analysis, therefore, we are fighting a lonely battle—we isolate ourselves because of our inability to believe in the good will of our neighbor.

Unscrupulous people are quick to exploit our latent distrust. The way of Iago with Othello has been reenacted countless times in the dramas of history as well as fiction. Without any foundation in fact, Iago was systematically able to undermine Othello's trust in his beloved Desdemona. He kept fanning the flames of the Moor's jealousy until Othello was beside himself with rage and strangled his unsuspecting wife. But long before Shakespeare wrote his tragedy, the people of Israel destroyed the friendship between Saul and David by chanting: "Saul has killed his thousands but David has killed his ten thousands." (I Sam. 18:7). Again, without any basis in fact, Saul began to suspect that David was plotting against him. He, too, attempted murder, but David dodged the javelin he hurled at him. On more than one occasion Saul realized that his suspicions were baseless but his own insecurity was too great to tolerate a leader as talented as David. Soon his suspicions were aroused once more and David had to flee for his life. Saul, like Othello, found it hard to believe in his own worth.

How easily we can threaten each other simply by being ourselves! In spite of our good intentions we appear to others as potential enemies. The only way to avoid this tension is to curtail our own self-expression. Harry Emerson Fosdick describes a college professor who took a friendly interest in a younger colleague and offered him counsel and encouragement. As soon as the younger man began to develop confidence and to stand on his own feet, the older man began to have misgivings. When the young professor went on to win wider popularity and larger elections to his courses than the professor himself, the older man's misgivings developed into an irrational and pathological jealousy. He convinced himself that the younger man was involved in a diabolical plot to undermine him.[8]

Wherever people are thrown together, we find the inevitable tensions. Every office force, school faculty, factory shift, athletic team, local congregation, service club and individual family has its share of internecine warfare, undercurrents of discontent and areas of tension. One has only to become involved within the group for any length of time to sense these undercurrents. The only groups that seem to escape are those that we observe from a distance.

Students who come to church colleges and even theological seminaries may become disillusioned after the first few months. They arrive with an idealistic picture of what a church college or a theological seminary is like, and soon discover the contrasting reality. Their disillusionment is over more than the institution; it is over life itself. Here they had hoped to find a group where the individuals involved were

---

[8] Fosdick, *op. cit.,* pp. 166-167.

better than they. Unhappily, they discover the same problems in the idealized group that they knew at home. They
find the same weaknesses in other students that they themselves have. Behind the accusations that they make against
the group lurks their own accusing conscience.

The bitterness of their disappointment shows how unrealistic their anticipation was. They had hoped the group
would give them something which they lacked. Now they
realize that it is they who must give something to the group,
and they doubt seriously that they can. It is disturbing to
realize that people-as-they-are, are similar to me-as-I-am.
Somewhere, we had hoped to find people without these
weaknesses. But now, we realize the truth of the statement:
I am as needed as I myself am in need.

Whenever we participate in group activities, there is the
possibility that we may hurt others just as they may hurt us.
The hostility that surges through us also surges through
others. Either we accept life as it is, and enter into it in
spite of the hazards, or we withdraw because the hazards are
too great. As Harry S Truman said, "If you can't stand the
heat, stay out of the kitchen." Yet what we fear in others
is latent also in ourselves—and how do you withdraw from
yourself?

6
CONSCIENCE ALWAYS ACCUSES

In the last chapter we looked into the workings of hostility. In this chapter we shall discuss the experience of guilt. Guilt and hostility are closely related. Both of them center in blaming—only the object of the blaming is different. The hostile person blames others and the guilty person blames himself. The difference however is not an absolute one, but is, rather, a difference between dominant and recessive characteristics. The person who blames others is dominantly hostile, but behind his hostility, in a recessive position, is guilt. In fact, the discomfiture of this guilt may instigate his hostility. The person who blames himself is dominantly guilty, but hostility is present and may even be a causative factor in his guilt. However, one thing stands out positively—the person who is actively hostile or guilty is not a passive person. He has a certain vitality even though the emotions that motivate him are negative. In his active blaming of himself or others, he is, by this very activity, attaching some importance to himself. He stands in contrast to those who repress these negative feelings and who thus suffer a loss in their sense of self-worth.

BUILT-IN PENAL SYSTEM

Any study of guilt leads inevitably to the conscience. The conscience is not only a built-in judge, but is also a built-in penal system. It is a distinctly human phenomenon which is constantly at work either "accusing or excusing" the person to whom it belongs. The standards by which the conscience accuses or excuses, vary with the culture as well as with the individual concerned, although there is a minimum common denominator. While some cultures have highly developed moral and ethical systems, and others have only a primitive code, they possess a certain degree of unanimity in moral codes.

A look at some ancient and modern cultures illustrates this universality. One of the most savage of the American Indian tribes, the Apaches, strangely enough, had a clearly defined moral code which governed the life of the tribe. While the savage Apache differed with the civilized Hebrew on from whom it was wrong to steal, for example, both agreed that it was wrong to steal from those within one's own group. Again, the Communists show by the kind of confessions they extort from their deviates that they adhere to some kind of ethical standards. They may claim that they have dispensed with the ethical nonsense of the bourgeois capitalist but they use something very similar to justify their own judgments.

Yet, our point is not the universality of any minimum code in moral standards, but the universality of a built-in penal system within the human being. Each person is under the judgment of his conscience in one way or another. He may rationalize his motives to bypass its accusations, or he may try to repress his conscience altogether. Some sabotage themselves to pacify their conscience. Others try to bribe their consciences with promises of future overcompensation. There are even those who project their self-accusations onto others, and blame them. Each of these ways is an attempt to dodge the direct accusation of conscience—to make it excuse rather than accuse. These ways are the "dead works" of conscience from which the letter to the Hebrews says Christ came to purge us (Heb. 9:14). Their effect is to "sear the conscience"—to burn off its sensitive edges (I Tim. 4:2).

The conscience is more responsive than we think. Beneath its cauterized surface its sensitivity continues to register. Rarely do we notice this sensitivity from a person's external behavior, for the person with the seared conscience may give the impression of having no conscience at all.

But the counselor usually sees these people in a different pose. In a counseling relationship, even those who seem most removed from an appearance of guilt, may let down their defenses, and in deep distress reveal their self-accusations. In their public relations these people feel they dare not show one vulnerable spot in their defensive armor lest they leave themselves wide open to attack. The way to help such people become aware of their needs is to accept them as they are. Only in this way can they see that nothing terrible will happen if they let down their guard.

If anyone is born without a conscience it would be the sociopath. In fact, society often has to confine the sociopath in jails or hospitals simply because he has no evident pattern of self-control. He impulsively acts out his desires without moral reflection. Yet what is least observable in the sociopathic personality—namely guilt—may play a large role in the disorder. The sociopath's only awareness of guilt comes during his rare moments of introspection. Only then does he feel vaguely uncomfortable. This discomfort antagonizes the basic meaninglessness of his existence. His response is one of quick escape into an unreflective and animal-like involvement with sensory experience.

Yet, even the sociopath's escape is not complete—his conscience still reacts to his behavior. Although neither he nor his observers are aware of it, a highly sensitive machine with a skilled human operator can pick up this reaction. Even the most hardened criminal cannot lie without specific and uncontrollable physiological reactions. The conscience always accuses!

A similar exposure may take place under hypnosis. Though an individual's normal countenance may be as impassive as the great stone face, he may behave quite differently under hypnosis. As the hypnotist directs him back to those occurrences when he felt guilt, the pain of this experience is shown by the contortions of his countenance. The sight is similar to the face of a person who is having a bad dream. In sleep, as in hypnosis, the public relations censor does not operate.

The counselor's challenge is to achieve this same harmony between the outer person and the inner one in the waking state. But he does not make contact with the real person behind the facade by probing for him. This would merely stiffen resistance. Rather, he tries to create an accepting atmosphere that encourages the counselee to realize that he, the counselor, is not judging him. Since there is no threat from without, the counselee may be emboldened to face the threat from within.

If I did not know better, the idea that I should try to exonerate myself before my own conscience would be comic. Imagine a trial in which the prosecuting attorney, the defense attorney, the defendant, the judge, and the flogger were all the same person, and you get an idea of the complexity of human nature. How then do we try to exonerate ourselves before our own conscience? The first try is usually on the grounds of ignorance: "I didn't know any better." This is how Socrates saw things. For him, sin was due to ignorance. The New Testament, however, disagrees. It claims that: "To him that knoweth to do good and doeth it not, to him it is sin" (James 4:17).

ASSUMPTION OF FREEDOM

When we can no longer substantiate our ignorance we turn to the excuse of impotency: "I had no opportunity to do otherwise." This excuse is to the point because the accusation of conscience assumes human freedom—the defendant cannot be convicted unless he is responsible for his actions. Was there a fork in the road where he could have made another turn? Or was there but one direction in which he could have gone? Whenever something goes wrong the cry goes up, "Whose fault is it?" "Who is to blame!" Almost instinctively our defenses go up. "Not I!" When there is blame, there is also punishment. Thus we have the urgent need to justify ourselves.

Occasionally, the instinctive need to justify ourselves takes a curious twist. Some people seem to want to take the blame. What causes them to seek punishment? Is this a reversal of our normal desire to avoid punishment? Actually it is not. The choice is not between punishment and no punishment, but between greater and lesser punishment. These people feel the accusation so strongly that assuming blame actually eases the painful tension. But even when it is defensive, the admission of guilt is still depressing.

The amount of energy we expend in self-exoneration shows how egocentric the accusations of conscience make us. Ironically, this very conscience, whose accusations stimulate egocentricity, turns around and condemns us for our egocentricity! The accusation of conscience is so much a matter within our own person that we rarely believe reassurances of our innocence which come from others. Their efforts to ease us may even make us feel more isolated in our guilt. We know that our guilt is an affair between me, myself and I; others are simply not privy to the facts.

The inescapable accusations of conscience are described by the Christian doctrine of original sin. The words "original sin" have a forbidding sound. We associate them with worn-out religious deprecations of man, but, they simply describe the principle upon which the familiar tension between my conscience and myself is based. The words are paradoxical—but so is the tension! The word *original* corresponds to our insistence that "it is not my fault." I am not responsible. The word *sin* means that it is my fault—that I am responsible. I am not free: the condition is part of me to begin with. But, I am free: the accusations of conscience will not let me off with the plea of impotence.

The age-old argument over whether man is free or predestined is inevitable because man is actually both. On the one hand, conscience judges man as if he were responsible; on the other hand, it frustrates him by demanding more than he can fulfill. Those romanticists, who exalt human freedom and ignore the constitutional and environmental infringements upon that freedom, often prepare the way for a totalitarian reaction in which individual freedom is eliminated. Totalitarian systems, however, cannot ignore individual responsibility. This inconsistency is illustrated by the absurdity of a Communist government which extracts confessions of guilt from individuals who are supposedly products of environmental influences.

It was this inconsistency that disturbed the last days of

Rubashov the central character of Arthur Koestler's *Darkness at Noon.* He had been a faithful party official when a change in the top leadership brought about his purge. As he awaited execution after being sentenced by a People's Court, he tried with the methodical logic of the disciplined intellect to find the equation for this inconsistency. But a factor was missing—the logic was simply inadequate.

> The Party denied the free will of the individual—and at the same time it exacted his willing self-sacrifice. It denied his capacity to choose between two alternatives—and at the same time it demanded that he should constantly choose the right one. It denied his power to distinguish good and evil—and at the same time it spoke pathetically of guilt and treachery. The individual stood under the sign of economic fatality, a wheel in a clockwork which had been wound up for all eternity and could not be stopped or influenced—and the Party demanded that the wheel should revolt against the clockwork and change its course. There was somewhere an error in the calculation: the equation did not work out.[1]

CREATION OF ANXIETY

Since the accusations of conscience assume human freedom, a misuse of this freedom constitutes a crime. Conscience not only pronounces judgment on this misuse of freedom, but also pronounces sentence. It is the sentence that is the real source of the anxiety in guilt. What is going to happen to me! This anxiety extends beyond the human to the divine, and beyond the temporal to the eternal. Its tremors are felt throughout our entire person. As Huck Finn put it, "Conscience takes up more room than all the

[1] (New York: The Macmillan Company, 1941), p. 257.

rest of a person's insides." Or as Fosdick phrased it: "The ideal confronts the actual," (the *should* confronts the *is*) "and taunts it."[2] Thus the *should* and the *is* are in continual tension with each other. Horney calls this tension the "tryanny of the should."[3] When we fail to convert *is* into *should,* we experience the sentence of condemnation and await the worst. Though the *worst* has repercussions for the future, it may also have its focus in the present.

A phobia is an example of how the entire process of anticipating retribution can be packed into a single situation. I was asked by a physician to counsel with a lady who had a phobia over cancer. In spite of repeated medical assurance that she had nothing organic wrong with her, she was convinced that she had cancer. This fear was constantly on her mind and every ache and pain gave her imagination renewed evidence. As I talked with her, she happened to remark that her father had died from cancer the previous year. When none of the other members of the family would care for the father during his illness, she received him into her home.

The way in which she spoke about the huge amount of care that her father had required, indicated that she had negative feelings toward him. Actually, she had taken him in begrudgingly, out of a sense of duty. Father and daughter had never gotten along well together, and she hoped that this gesture on her part might win her father's affection. But even as she cared for him, he made no effort to conceal his preference for another daughter.

She became increasingly resentful of the fact that she had to care for him and began to wish that he would die. She finally sent him to the hospital against his will. Much to

---

[2] Fosdick, *op. cit.,* p. 53.
[3] Horney, *op. cit.*

everybody's surprise, he died within a few days. "If I could have known that he had only a few days to live," she moaned, "I would not have sent him. Maybe I hastened his death. God was probably punishing me because I—I even prayed that he would die." Small wonder that physical examinations brought her no reassurance. Her guilty conscience had convinced her that God would punish her for her attitude toward her father by consigning her to the same kind of fate. It was the law of just desert!

Psychoanalyst Theodore Reik describes a similar origin to his own pre-disposition to panic. He relates that once, when his seven-year-old daughter did not return home at her regular time from school, he experienced complete panic. He imagined all sorts of terrible things happening to her, and soon was no longer able to stand his anxiety. He cancelled his appointments and headed for the police station. When he arrived, he was told by the police that his little girl had returned home after visiting a friend. On hearing the news he broke into uncontrollable sobs. As he shook the policeman's hand he had a strong desire to kiss it, and all the way home, he kept doubting that she was really safe.

Later he was both embarrassed and perplexed by his behavior. Why had he acted so irrationally? Forcing himself to analyze his actions, he finally resurrected a painful memory. It seems that when he and his famly were stranded in Holland following their escape from Austria during the Nazi occupation, his wife told him she was pregnant. The news gave him no joy for it simply added to his already heavy burdens. Then, when the family took refuge in the United States, he often wished the child would not be born. As soon as he realized what he had been wishing, he would immediately ban the thought from his mind. But there were emotional repercussions. In the seven intervening years, fear lingered in his mind that something would happen to the child as a punishment for his wish. Although Reik refers to himself as an "infidel Jew" he describes his feelings in the following religious terms:

> There had been vague suspicions in me that when things took a turn for the better the unknown power would retaliate, and I would be punished for those old wishes which I unconsciously considered thought crimes. The police station must have been in my thought the place of Judgment Day, where I would hear the verdict. I had, it seemed, no trust in a forgiving or kind God or destiny, which would forget and forgive my sins of thought.[4]

Obviously one does not have to be conscious of any religious beliefs to experience the judgment of guilt and the fear of retribution. They are not the result of being religious but of being human. Once our conscience is disturbed, we can become the victim of all manner of irrational fears.

LOSS OF SELF-RESPECT

Sigmund Freud believed that these fears are due to a conflict between the superego and the id. The id represents the spontaneous desires which are primarily associated with our biological appetites. The superego represents the restraints of society which have become part of us. The third element, the ego, has to resolve the conflict. If we want to be accepted by society, we must obey the superego, and thwart our natural desires. If we follow our natural desires,

---

[4] *The Secret Self* (New York: Farrar, Straus & Cudahy, Inc., 1953), p. 312.

we are free to an extent; but we lose the love of society. Freud believed that most people who suffer from neuroses possess egos which have sided with the superego against the id, an alignment which has failed to satisfy them.

When we fulfill a role we think others expect of us, we become increasingly unaware of who we really are. Willy Loman in the play *Death of a Salesman,* is an excellent example of a man who suffers from the loss of his identity. Willy was a salesman of the old school with a line a mile long and a front just as high. Willy was convinced that he knew how to be liked and how to sell. But Willy began to lose his touch. He was out of date, and he was too rigid to recognize it. The formula had worked before, and it would work again! He just knew that! He was wrong: it failed! Willy was through as a salesman—and that was not supposed to happen. His world collapsed. There was nothing left for him to do but to face what he really was. This confrontation proved too much for his ego—and he committed suicide. As he was being laid to rest, his wife spoke his obituary: "He didn't know who he was."[5]

Or, did he know too well? Socrates, the sage who said, "know thyself," also said that sin is ignorance. Perhaps we need illusions about ourselves in order to live comfortably with ourselves. The accusations of conscience can be severe enough to destroy our self-respect, and conformance to the dictates of the superego often fails to stop these accusations. The realm of thoughts and feelings remains outside the discipline of the superego. Indeed, in our thoughts and feelings we may even be rebelling against the superego— we resent having to live a role in order to be accepted. We resent it as a restriction on our freedom and rebel inwardly.

---

[5] Arthur Miller, *Death of a Salesman* (New York: Viking Press, Inc., 1949).

If the people whom we are trying to please knew our thoughts and feelings, they might be shocked. Could they possibly love us then?

This very question increases our tension. To make matters worse our conscience now accuses us of hypocrisy: our *outer* appearance is merely a coverup for our *inner* actuality. Therefore, there is more guilt. If there is more guilt, there is more to hide, and more fear over whether that which is hidden will stay hidden. In consequence, we erect more defenses to protect us even from ourselves—or to justify ourselves in case we are threatened. We endure all these tortuous machinations to avoid being exposed as insincere. For if we are insincere, we are worthless—and lose all respect in our own eyes and in the eyes of others.

There seems to be more to this loss of self-respect than the conflict between the id and superego with which the ego must contend. Goethe's *Faust* struggles with this same internal conflict and comes to the conclusion he has two souls:

> Two souls, alas! are lodg'd within my breast,
>   Which struggle there for undivided reign;
> One to the world, with obstinate desire,
>   And closely—cleaving organs still adheres;
> Above the mist, the other doth aspire,
>   With sacred vehemence, to purer spheres.[6]

But when judgment is passed, it is passed not only on one of the souls, but on the total person. When Isaiah was confronted by the reality of the presence of God, his immediate response was, "Woe is me, for I am undone!" (Isa. 6:5).

---

[6] J. W. von Goethe, *Faust,* etc., Vol. 19, The Harvard Classics (New York: P. F. Collier & Son Co., 1909), p. 46.

When Simon Peter, against his own better judgment, let down his nets at Jesus' behest, he caught so many fish he had to call for help in order to keep his net from breaking and his boat from sinking. Overcome by this same sense of unworthiness he said, "Depart from me, O Lord, for I am a sinful man." (Luke 5:8). Also pertinent are the words of John Masefield's penitent sinner, "The harm I've done being me."[7]

Here is a guilt not over an id, or a lower nature or even a lower soul, but a guilt over the total self. When guilt reaches these proportions it becomes despair. Of all psychic pains there is none more unbearable than despair. Even when the sharp awareness and specific content of such a guilt are repressed, a dull, vague sort of apathy remains in the deeper recesses of our awareness. This is the buffer zone which protects us from the intolerable despair.

Beside the pain of judgment and the fear of the consequences, there is also a wounded pride in our guilt. We would like to think more highly of ourselves than we do, but we cannot! This is particularly aggravating because guilt over a wounded pride is not the kind of guilt you can express before God. He is not the One who is offended. And for this there is also guilt. We suffer guilt because of our guilt. Here is the frustration—the bitterness—the despair —from which we run.

---

[7] *Quoted in* Fosdick, *op. cit.,* p. 200.

7
WHY CHRISTIANITY IS RESISTED

When Jesus visited His home town of Nazareth, He attended the synagogue service on the Sabbath. According to custom the rabbi asked Him to present the lesson for the day. He read the appointed scripture from the prophet Isaiah: "The Spirit of the Lord God is upon me, because the Lord has anointed me to bring good tidings to the afflicted; he has sent me to bind up the broken-hearted, to proclaim liberty to the captives and the opening of prison to those who are bound: to proclaim the year of the Lord's favor." As He finished reading He said, "Today this scripture has been fulfilled in your hearing" (Luke 4:16-30). In other words, He claimed to be the One whom the Lord had anointed to do these things. From the description of the task to which He set himself, Jesus came to do something about the human predicament we have been describing. But, his hometown couldn't believe in Him. To them He was simply Joseph's son whom they had known as a child.

Good News

The people of Nazareth resisted Jesus' claims because they thought they knew Him too well. They wanted no part of whatever He had to give because they were offended that one of their own number would make such claims. Yet the resistance to Jesus and his message goes beyond a home-town irritation. Nazareth only symbolized an universal re-action—a resistance that is indigenous to human nature. On the basis of our perception of this human nature, we are in a position to see why the Gospel of Christ is re-sisted—why it is offensive to us.

The word *Gospel* is from the Old English word *Godspel* which means good tale or good news. Why should anyone want to resist good news? Whether news is good or not depends upon one's expectations. This particular good news conflicts with any adjustment to life that is based upon a defense system. We can see, therefore, why the good news may not be good news, even to those who consider them-selves to be religious. The good news of Christ applies specifically to those things about us from which we are running—to those things about us that condemn us. To receive this good news means that we must face the un-complimentary side of our personality, and do so without self-justification.

Such self-confrontation runs counter to our desire to think more highly of ourselves. We want improvement and the Gospel offers us acceptance. We want approval from others and the Gospel offers us forgiveness. When our fore-most desire is to elevate the mental image others have of us, of what significance is forgiveness? Who needs it? Obviously we cannot be expected to buy something in which we have little interest. Does forgiveness bypass our basic wants? Or are we simply not ready for it?

Before we are ready for the good news, we have to be ready to give up our built-in defense system, and this is no small matter. Some of us may be aware that the very act of receiving the good news could create an internal revolution by bringing about the collapse of all our supporting props. And such a collapse could have disastrous consequences—and not only in the way we anticipate.

Another episode in Jesus' life demonstrates these consequences. The Pharisee who invited Jesus to dinner and the uninvited woman who anointed His feet while he reclined at the table are contrasted (Luke 7:36-50). Since private dinners were open to the public in the New Testament times, an uninvited guest usually created no stir. But this particular uninvited guest did. The Pharisee had invited Jesus in the belief that He was a prophet, and he thought that Jesus was unaware of the fact that this woman was a woman of the streets. He reasoned that Jesus would have refused her overture, had He but known of her occupation. If He did not know it, how then could He be a prophet?

Knowing the conflict that this incident was creating in the Pharisee's mind, Jesus presented him with this parable: A certain man had two debtors—one who owed him a large amount and another who owed him a small amount. When neither could pay, he forgave them both. Now which of the two would love him more? The Pharisee was forced to acknowledge, "The one, I suppose, to whom he forgave more." The point was obvious. The woman had faced up to herself in a way that the Pharisee had not. Therefore, her ties with Christ were much more intimate.

Giving and receiving go together. The woman was already giving. What the Pharisee could not understand was that she was also receiving. To make the point clear Jesus said in the presence of them all, "Your sins are forgiven." He did not say this for the woman's sake—she knew it all the time. It was this that moved her with tears and ointment to anoint His feet. It was said for the sake of the Pharisee who had failed to offer his guest the water in which to wash His feet (a common courtesy in that age). Perhaps we have a clue in this story of why love is so lacking in our midst— and also why defensiveness and self-justification are so prominent. We can see now why the Pharisee is always with us.

OMNIPRESENT PHARISEE

The Pharisees were a religious and political party in Palestine and were Jesus' leading opponents. They still are. Though they no longer exist as an official group, their spirit is always with us. The logic of the Pharisee is very familiar. The woman was bad company. A respectable man ought not to be seen with her in good company. Of course, if he is away from home and such women are part of the entertainment, that is a different matter. What one may indulge in for diversion, in a clandestine escapade, must never be confused with one's public image.

The woman erred because she wasted precious ointment. The ointment was very expensive. She had obviously sacrificed to buy it. Think of all the good causes to which this money could have been given. Instead she sentimentally "blew it" on an impractical, if not nonsensical, demonstration of devotion. The woman was neither respectable nor practical, and therefore she should have been dismissed. The Pharisee is always with us because he is in us.

The Pharisee's main obsession is to qualify. To accomplish this, he attempts to emphasize something acceptable about himself and to soft pedal something not so acceptable. That the Pharisees as individuals and as a group, were successful in their efforts, is attested by Jesus' caustic description of them as mausoleums, white and glistening on the outside, but full of decay and rotting bones within (Matt. 23:27). In spite of our judgment upon the Pharisees, we do the same thing. Only our method is different.

The old method of the Pharisee has been ruined. We cannot lift holy hands to God in public places and pray aloud that we are thankful that we are not as other men— that we give generously to charity and the church and that we conduct ourselves decently and in order. In his denunciations of those first century Pharisees, Jesus destroyed this method once and for all. If we attempted to follow it we would be labeled as conceited. Such obvious boasting would be socially unacceptable. Anyone who indulged in it would be considered a boor. He would find himself socially rejected as a braggart. Most of us have enough sense to realize this.

But when you destroy a method, you do not necessarily destroy the spirit behind the method. Blocked in one mode of expression, the spirit seeks out another. And, we have found a better method. We have discovered that you do not have to build yourself up to achieve status—you merely have to tear others down. This gives you the same effect. We have become experts in confessing other people's sins, or rather in pronouncing judgment on other people's sins. Either openly or covertly, we systematically lower the people's stature by criticizing them to others And in the same operation, we are elevating our own stature. We are saying in effect, "I would not do things as this person does. I would not be this kind of person. The fact that I can pronounce this judgment upon him indicates this. Therefore, I am better than this person." The judge is always on top! This method is considered quite acceptable in our day. Indeed, it is widely used even in so-called Christian circles.

We can also achieve status by apologizing for ourselves. We hope that somebody else will build us up. "I'm no good," we say.

"Oh, yes you are," says our friend.

"Oh, no I'm not," we persist. "I can't do anything right."

"Now don't talk that way," he replies in agitation.

"Well, it's true," we go on, "so why deny it."

"Listen," says our friend, "stop running yourself down. There are a lot of fine things about you."

"No there are not," we counter with rising interest.

"There are so!" he says.

"What for example," we ask, cupping our ear.

Children learn this technique early as a way of avoiding punishment. They discover that people rarely attack someone who has already wounded himself. A six-year-old playmate of my daughter asked me the time one day. "It's five o'clock," I answered.

"Oh," she said, "I was supposed to be home by four o'clock."

I saw that she was upset, and I asked if there was anything I could do.

"Mommy will be mad at me," she said. "She told me I would get a spanking if I was not home by four o'clock." Suddenly she looked relieved. "I know what I'll do. I'll cry first. Mommy never spanks me, if I cry first."

We learn early that if we criticize ourselves first, even those who are about to criticize us will probably say nice encouraging words instead. This type of self-depreciation is a kind of egocentricity, rather than a genuine expression of the defeat of our ego. It is a camouflaged way of "fishing for compliments," while we create the impression that we are modest and humble. Some people even make a virtue out of admitting their faults. This is probably their reaction to Jesus' condemnation of the boasting of the Pharisees, but the effect is the same—they bring glory to themselves.

The virtues of modesty and humility rate high in our society—particularly in Christian circles. If we can impress others that we possess these virtues, our reputation is enhanced. Did Jesus not say that we should humble ourselves and take the lowest seats? Did He not condemn the Pharisees who have always exalted themselves and preempted the highest seats? (Luke 14:7-11) He certainly did, but He meant what He said in the context of His culture. He was criticizing those who were exalting themselves and despising others. In today's culture, it is possible to take the lowest seat in order to exalt ourselves and to despise those who take the highest seats. Ours is a peculiar society which allows a person to exalt himself by lowering himself, but such is the ingenuity of the pharisaical spirit. We all status-seek to a certain extent, and if modesty has top priority as a status elevator, we want others to think we are modest. Of course honesty may be a casualty in all of this self-effacement—we are evidently quite disappointed if our friend should agree rather than argue with our self-depreciations.

There are many ways to the top. For some people the more disguised the way is, the better. While at a party for writers, Thomas Mann was introduced to a particular writer for whom the occasion was quite overwhelming. "Oh, Mr. Mann," he said, "I don't deserve even to be at this party, let alone to meet you. You are a great writer and I—well I am just a hack."

Later Thomas Mann said, "That fellow had no right to make himself so small. He is not that big!"

The Protestant Reformation insisted, among other things, that no one could be saved by his good works. This idea has since been hammered home in the churches of the Reformation. Again, one can stop a method without stopping the intent; the desire to qualify simply finds another mode of expression. Blocked in the use of good works, a Protestant may use what Paul Tillich calls "negative" or "emotional" works to qualify. He prays: "Oh God, I am devoid of all goodness. I despise myself for my sins. I am very sorry and penitent. In fact I feel perfectly miserable. Now do I qualify? Now am I worthy of forgiveness—of deliverance from harm and danger —and of other divine blessings?" The person who prays this way seems to fear that if he is too happy, something will go wrong to balance things. Therefore he must make it clear that he has his share of suffering, even if it is self-inflicted. His motto is: "Don't laugh too hard or you may soon be crying."

The need to impress others with our redeeming qualities extends also to God. I recall seeing a cartoon in which three convicts were breaking rocks. One stood apart from the other two and had a pained and pious look upon his face. The two were looking askance in his direction as the one said to the other: "I can't stand his guiltier-than-thou attitude." Yes indeed, there are many ways to the top!

THE UNKNOWN GOD

When St. Paul visited Athens to bring the Athenians his good news, he was much disturbed by what he found in that ancient seat of Hellenic culture. Shrine after shrine had been erected to the various gods—Petronius, the Roman satirist, said that "it was easier to find a god than a man in Athens." Naturally the visiting Jew noticed the many shrines, but he was especially interested in the altar the Athenians had erected to "an unknown God." Perhaps it was not only the fear that one had been omitted, but rather in all of their efforts to communicate with the Divine, that they had missed Him.

At any rate this shrine to an unknown God gave Paul his opening. He had aroused the Athenian's curiosity by conversing with them in the market place, and they invited him to the Areopagus, their official debating place, to hear what he had to say. There he told them that he had noticed they were very religious because of their many shrines. Then he mentioned their altar to an unknown God. "What therefore you worship as unknown," he said, "this I proclaim to you" (Acts 17:16-34, R.S.V.).

Paul's "unknown God" is still unknown. The Athenians were unique only in their elaborate attempt to avoid what they feared. Even among the religious there is always the possibility that God is unknown. Perhaps it is inevitable that the Divine must always elude the human. Or as Paul put it in his address in the Areopagus, "The God who made the world and everything in it, being Lord of heaven and earth, does not live in shrines made by man, nor is He served by human hands as though He needed anything, since He himself gives to all men life and breath and everything." He said this within sight of the colossal statue of Athene, and he was addressing a people who regarded these religious works of art as the highest glory of their city.

Tillich calls the unknown God in our culture the "God above God."[1] He is the God above the God we picture in our minds, not only in our works of art. It is He who finds us rather than we who find Him. He breaks into our consciousness to reveal Himself. But this is no smooth operation. Our mental image of God is in the way. It is as much an idol as

---

[1] *The Courage To Be* (New Haven: Yale University Press, 1952), p. 182.

is an image of stone. The God above God must break through this obstacle—and this means an internal upheaval. Something definitely happens to us and we know it.

The Christian teaching concerning man is that he was created in God's image. From a realistic point of view it may be just as true to say that man has created God in his own image much in the manner described by J. B. Phillips in his book, *Your God Is Too Small.*[2] But the God we have fashioned is more than just small—He is distorted. We distort Him not only because we are human, but because we ourselves are distorted. Having lost the divine image in which we were created, we attempt to create a God in our own image. So we resist the God above our created god.

The Youth Research Center is an organization that has conducted scientific research of church youth over the past several years. The results indicate that the major problem of these young people is their low self-image, or as it is interpreted in older terms, uncertainty of acceptance or forgiveness. Even those among the youth who understood the doctrine of forgiveness at least intellectually, indicated little correlation in their lives between this knowledge and a charitable attitude toward others. Again, this conflicts with the teaching that love grows out of forgiveness. Since the chief concern of these youth was over their self-image, they were in doubt about whether others really liked them, and this doubt contributed to their low opinion of themselves. Their uncertainty over their own worth and their apprehension over how others rated them harmonized with their uncertainty over God's forgiveness and their lack of charity toward others.

Is the gospel message relevant for this day and age of impersonal relationships? Can its message penetrate the

---

[2] (New York: The Macmillan Company, 1954).

protective barriers we create to surround and compartmentalize our lives? Unless and until that message breaks through, its meaning and power are remote and inert. The oft heard criticism that religion is not being communicated effectively is partly true. It is equally true that some who hear and understand the message are quite unwilling to respond in terms of personal commitment.

8
THE
WAY UP
IS DOWN

The problem over the good news of Christianity may not be that we fail to recognize it as good news, but that we recognize it as news that is too good. It may be too high for us. Soren Kierkegaard compared the good news to an emperor who wanted to do something for one of his serfs. Confronting the man he said, "Come, marry my daughter. Be my son-in-law. Live in my palace and sit at my table."

The poor peasant shook his head. No—this was too much—it would make him too uncomfortable. "If you want to do something for me," he said, "give me a plot of ground that I can farm and a house of my own and I will be satisfied. But to want to make me your son-in-law, to live in your palace and eat at your table—no, this is too much. It makes too much of what it is to be me. It makes too much of what it is to be a man."[1]

We too may be reluctant to receive all that God wants to

---

[1] *Sickness unto Death*, pp. 215-216.

give us. We would prefer that God bless us as we are, rather than get too involved with God Himself. The involvement demanded by the good news can be frightening. Like the emperor's offer to the peasant, it would obligate us to the Giver—make us beholden. To become the emperor's son-in-law and sit at his table, the peasant would have to face his own unworthiness. He would also have to become a representative of the emperor's family. The offer of "too much" creates anxiety because it also creates demands. It forces a person to evaluate himself and thus throws him in upon his guilt. Thus, the offer of "too much" leads to despair as much as the offer of "too little." It obligates us, and therefore cuts into our freedom.

History has shown that this disquieting quality of the good news can easily be adjusted. We can put the new wine into old wineskins, but since the old wineskins will not hold new wine, the attempt results in the loss of the new wine. Thus, instead of permitting religion to upset our defense system, we can take it into our defense system. We have seen how this can be done when we examined the methods of the Pharisee. He uses religion as one of several ways to demonstrate his redeeming qualities. We can also take religion into our defense system by accepting it as a blank check from some distant and wealthy relative. That is what Dietrich Bonhoeffer calls cheap rather than free grace. We cheapen the good news when we no longer think of it as a relationship, but as a bank account. Says Bonhoeffer, "Cheap grace means grace as a doctrine, a principle, a system. It means forgiveness of sins proclaimed as a general truth, the love of God taught as the Christian 'conception' of God. An intellectual assent to that idea is held to be of itself sufficient to secure remissions of sins."[2]

---

[2] *The Cost of Discipleship* (New York: The Macmillan Company, 1948), p. 37.

Obviously, when the good news is reduced to ideas and principles, it creates very few obligations. It has all the characteristics of the last will and testament of an indulgent and deceased old grandfather. Therefore, as Bonhoeffer says, it offers a cheap covering for sin: "no contribution is required, still less any real desire to be delivered from sin."[3] The way to avoid the threat in the good news is to reduce the personal dimension within which it is given, and substitute instead the dimension of ideas. If we turn the good news into the business atmosphere of a good deal, we can be released from the obligation of "being bought with a price" (I Cor. 6:20).

We are the products of our economically minded age and seek a return greater than our investment. This is the basis of good business. If we can work out an arrangement with God in which we get the better of the deal, we are delighted —provided that we do not get too personally involved in the process. The fellow who has made a deal is free. If he gets too involved, personally, then he may not be free. This is the way it is with the good news. "You are not your own," says the apostle, "you were bought with a price" (I Cor. 6:19-20). But we want to be our own, and cheap grace offers a way out of our dilemma.

As a counselor I have repeatedly witnessed the escape of cheap grace. A good example was the young couple who came to me for advice. They sat nervously before me as they talked about getting married and were obviously the products of cheap grace. They wanted to get married immediately, they said and fidgeted. Their lack of ease pointed up their guilt feelings, for taking the young man aside, I asked him if his girl friend was pregnant. Visibly disturbed by the question he stammered out: "I—I don't think so."

---

[3] *Ibid.*, p. 37.

"In other words," I said, "you have had sexual relations together."

He hung his head and spoke an almost inaudible "Yes."

After we had talked about the situation a bit, I asked him if he was reconciled to God over this problem. "That's the trouble," he said. "I've always been told you could get forgiveness for anything just by asking for it."

"How is that trouble?" I asked.

"It makes it too easy," he said. "You think, 'I know I can be forgiven—so . . .'"

"Does this reduce the incentive to follow through on your principles?" I asked.

"That's right," he said, "It's too easy, it doesn't seem to mean anything. It makes a farce of forgiveness."

Cheap grace causes us to lose respect for Christianity. Knowing we have abused God's offer, we no longer take His offer seriously. Any presentation of the Gospel that begins "All you have to do is . . ." perverts the Gospel. Instead of leading the receiver to a devotion to the Giver, it leads him to an abuse of the gift. "All-you-have-to-do" suggests a minimizing of responsibility. By the time the deal has been spelled out, the responsibility has been eliminated altogether.

A student pastor was counseling an inmate of a reformatory who felt very depressed over the trouble he had brought upon his parents. "I don't deserve all that my folks have done for me," he said. "They sure must love me a lot, but look what I've done. I don't deserve it. I'm no good."

The student asked, "You mean you just can't see anything good in yourself at all?"

"No, I can't," the boy answered. "Look at all the trouble I've caused."

The student pastor asked him: "Do you know that God loves you and will accept you as you are?"

"Oh, yes, I've been taught that," said the inmate. "I've

always thought that God would even forgive a person who waited to ask Him for forgiveness on his death bed. I figured that I could do this too; that I could do whatever I wanted just once more, and He'd forgive me." Once he had exploited the good news as a good deal, he could no longer take it seriously.

We are all in collusion to safeguard our respective ego defenses. This mutual assistance pact enables us to avoid issues that threaten to upset our defense system. Each one of us has had enough experience with a shaky defense to know the fear it causes. Were our defenses to fall, we would be thrown into despair. And the sorrow of despair is frightening because it is sorrow without hope. Tillich goes so far as to say that "all human life can be interpreted as a continuous attempt to avoid despair."[4] Perhaps we know of people who don't seem to fit this description; but who can judge the security of another person by his external appearance?

Experience in group work indicates that the potential for disturbance lies within us all. The unstructured nature of group therapy, for example, is enough in itself to unnerve most of us. We often preserve our security by working things out ahead of time, so that we are ready for what is coming. But when there is no structure, how can you ready yourself? The very silence that may dominate a group session is hard to endure. Normally, we are not accustomed to silence when we are with people. Talking relieves the tension of the interpersonal association.

The exchange that takes place in group therapy is unlike that of a social conversation. The members do not support each other's defense systems for their goal is honest communication. The members of the group grow confident

---

[4] *The Courage To Be,* p. 56.

enough to say what they think, even about each other. They may even question their own as well as other's motives— something normally off limits in social conversation. The whole therapy experience can "rock the boat," and participants may be more shaken than they thought possible. The fact that we can be upset by a group that which, though honest, is still accepting, shows why we rarely risked such honesty in our normal social intercourse.

The conversation in the counseling relationship is also quite different from social conversation. The counselor watches for signs of uneasiness. Instead of trying to relieve this uneasiness by avoiding it, he brings it out in the open by focusing on it. The counselor may introduce subjects that he knows are disturbing to the counselee in an effort to provide him with the support he needs to face these threats. He confronts him with realities that the counselee would otherwise ignore. In so doing, he anticipates the life process. For life can be a hard teacher, and sometimes its lessons prove disastrous. The counselor tries to prevent this from happening by providing an empathetic environment for the crumbling defenses of the counselee.

Crumbling defenses can be most disturbing. When we let down our defenses we, in a sense, surrender. It is the sort of surrender that takes place when we receive the good news. Upon receiving this news, the human spirit surrenders to the Spirit of God. It is this surrender that cheap grace would avoid. It is because this surrender is necessary that the good news is resisted.

CRISES AND GROWTH

Life is geared in the direction of crises. In its very character, there is what Kunkel calls, "the ultimatum to grow up or perish."[5] Smiley Blanton says it is "love or perish."[6] Centuries ago the prophet Amos declared "Thus saith the Lord. . . Seek ye Me and ye shall live" (Amos 5:4). Here is a view of life that gives direction to history.

The idea that life is pushing us in the direction of growth also gives a purpose to our personal history. This contrasts vividly with our contemporary anxiety over the meaninglessness of life.

In the New Testament there are two words for time: *chronos,* which means time as quantity, and *kairos,* which stands for time as quality. When St. Paul referred to the coming of the good news he said, "In the fullness of time God sent forth his son," (Gal. 4:4). The fullness of time (quantity) is a qualitative event (*kairos*). So each of us has his times—when life confronts him with an opportunity for growth. The intensity of the kairos opens him to receive.

We can stave off moments of crisis by running from them, but life pushes us until more and more drastic escapes become necessary. Some people turn to alcohol as a haven. Since it helps them to escape by dulling their sensitivities, they fail to realize that it may go on to create a delusional type of confidence. The alcoholic has escaped his *kairos* by creating a private world in which he is king. His is the state of mind which has been deluded by wishful thinking. He says, "Peace, peace, when there is no peace" (Jeremiah 6:14).

The alcoholic may prefer his delusional world to that of reality, even when his alcoholic escape leads him to a mental hospital. As one patient told the hospital chaplain: "Say, you fellows must get pretty disgusted with us alcoholics. We can

[5] *In Search of Maturity* (New York: Charles Scribner's Sons, 1952), p. 192.
[6] *Love or Perish* (New York: Simon & Schuster, Inc., 1956).

lie and deceive everyone, including ourselves. I'm not sure I'll make it this time. A lot of alcoholics say they want to quit, but they really don't mean it way down deep. They sort of crave the stuff and love it! In fact, I don't know if I can do it either. I don't really know if I want to quit. Right now I do, but. . . ."

That last word "but" is his honest admission that he is not ready to stop. Alcoholics Anonymous waits for the elimination of the "but." They wait for the alcoholic to hit bottom— and by *bottom* they mean the *kairos* when the situation created by his drinking is so serious that it overcomes his desire to escape. Sometimes AA does more than wait. At an AA convention I heard a member, who happened to be a clergyman, describe the way an AA member of his congregation had helped him to hit bottom. This man knew about the minister's problem and was determined to help him. But he had to proceed carefully since the minister, like other alcoholics, thought no one knew of his addiction—an illusion typical of the lack of reality in the alcoholic's world.

The church member invited the minister to his home and proceeded to get him drunk. Later he took him to a tavern where he got into a fight and had to be forcibly evicted. The member then took him back to his home and put him to bed. The next morning he confronted the minister with the evidence and suggested that he attend an AA meeting. When the clergyman arrived at the meeting, he could not raise his eyes for fear of whom he would see. When he finally looked up, he saw seven members of his own congregation. "We've been waiting for you for a long time," they said.

Human beings are characterized by inertia. Once we are stopped, we are hard to start; once we are started, we are hard to stop. The crises in our life counteract this inertia. They cause the old to collapse so that the new can be established. We resist our *kairos* because we have not yet suffered enough. We may be in a rut and hate it, but the rut is home —we are familiar with it. "No one after drinking old wine desires new, for he says, 'The old is good'" (Luke 5:39). There is security in familiarity, while the unknown is frightening. "Old slaves prefer to remain slaves." The security of the old must be shaken before we are ready to enter the new. Thus God directs the course of man's life in such a way that it fulfills His good purposes.

The Way Up is Down

I once heard a minister say that salvation means feeling at home in the universe. His implication was that feeling at home in the universe is not something that comes to us naturally. First, there has to be a breach—an estrangement —between us and the universe which forces us to build defenses. Then we must be sufficiently disturbed to become aware of the tension between what *ought* to be and what *is*. At this point, we are ready to listen to the words of John the Baptist, the prophet who prepares the way for the coming of the Messiah. He makes us acutely aware of the reality that we are homeless in the universe. Our defenses have attached us to lesser gods or idols. His task is to upset our trust in these objects of belief that rival the God who is above these gods. Stripped of our defenses, we reach the bottom. Here we realize that, without the God who is above other gods, we can do nothing. We come smack up against the reality from which we normally run. Sensing its nearness, we flee in fear. We are afraid to face God the way we are: without any covering for our nakedness or any distraction for our uneasiness.

I have counseled several people who were atheists, but

only on one occasion have I counseled someone who had a passionate desire to *be* an atheist. He was a young man who had been brought up in a church-going family. He had regularly attended the Sunday School and was active in the young people's group. Now, I can understand someone who is an atheist, but I had a difficult time understanding someone who *wanted* to be an atheist. I asked him why he had this desire.

"Oh, that's easy," he explained. "When I get to thinking there is no God, I get the most peaceful feeling I have ever known until—"

"Until what," I asked.

"Until I begin having my doubts—maybe He *is*."

"Then what?" I asked.

"Then," he said, "I get all tightened up inside—I just fill up with anxiety."

"Do you have any idea why?" I asked.

"Unfortunately I do," he said. "If there is a God, then I am AWOL."

Here is a psychological basis for a good deal of unbelief. If we can get rid of God, we can at least have the illusion that we have rid ourselves of guilt. Some religious people would like to get rid of God. They are religious only because they cannot count God out. They think they must pacify Him, but this is only their second choice. Evidently Martin Luther must have experienced this feeling at one time because he so clearly put his finger on the dilemma. "For a heart completely cast down," he said, "and in despair cannot open its mouth so wide, but it is dumb, or it slanders God and cannot think, believe or speak of God other than as a fearful tyrant, or as of the Devil and only wants to flee and get away from him. Yes it would that God were not

God, so that he might not suffer such things from him."[7]

But, God is difficult to eliminate. Like the young man who wanted to be an atheist, we still have our doubts. The thought that God *is* caused him to become disturbed, and disturbed he had become. The necessary avenue to God is to despair over ourselves before Him—to stand transparent before Him—and to say with the prophet, "Against thee, thee only, have I sinned" (Isa. 51:4). The breach must be faced before healing can take place. Before we find our home in the universe, we must be confronted by our homelessness. The way up is down.

[7] Gordon Rupp, *The Righteousness of God* (New York: Philosophical Library, 1953), p. 112.

9

GOD
COMES TO US

When we hit bottom the way opens for the God-above-God to enter the picture. The crisis itself creates the need for a Deliverer. Things have gone wrong, there seems no way out, and we suffer. Instead of harmony there is disharmony. The thread of meaning, which was holding life in place, is broken. In the middle of this collapse we ask ourselves why? Why did it happen—why did it happen *to me?* What is wrong with me? Not only do we ask what it is all worth; we ask what am *I* worth? The very collapse seems to be a judgment—a condemnation.

And what can I do about it? is the taunting question. Nothing! The bottom means defeat. Our resources are gone, and, this is the biggest revelation of all, we are beat. Help, if there is any, will have to come from outside. In this sense we can say that the ego dies. It succumbs with the cry: "Oh wretched man that I am, who shall deliver me from this body of death?" (Rom. 7:24) What has died is not our worst self, but our best. Our resources have been dissipated because the self we were proud of has met defeat. It is the whole of us—including even our righteous self—which has hit bottom.

AT THE BOTTOM—LOVE

As painful as it is to be broken down in this manner, it is necessary before we can be genuinely rebuilt. The fact that we can look critically at ourselves does not mean that only part of us has been broken down. That I can be both subject and object does not contradict my own wholeness. If one part of me is simply passing judgment upon another, then a little patchwork ought to restore the balance. Nothing genuinely new, however, comes out of patchwork. Additions are simply made to the old, and thus there is no essential change. It is a new garment that is needed and not new patches on the old (Luke 5:36).

In the Bible the disease of leprosy was used as an analogy for sin. Although the term was served as a loose description of several skin diseases, it included the disease we know as leprosy. In Biblical times lepers were isolated as unclean, and the healing of leprosy was called cleansing. The disease slowly encroached on its victim, destroying parts of the body before it climaxed in death. These characteristics made leprosy a meaningful symbol for sin.

In our day, the illnesses most helpful as analogies for sin are alcoholism and drug dependency. Not only are they as common today as leprosy was in ancient times, but their dominion over their victims is similar to sin's dominion. Victory comes only when the victim, enslaved and defeated, cries out for help. Like the sinner, the alcoholic or addict must accept responsibility for himself, helpless as he may be. Alcoholism, and some drug addictions, seem to have a physiological basis; yet the total person needs to become involved for recovery from the dependency.

When we hit bottom we expect the worst; instead we find love. It is then that the Holy Spirit declares Christ unto us (John 16:15). The Christian teaching of the Trinity has always been a challenge for speculation. How can God be one God and yet be three persons? While speculation upon the Trinity can be a fascinating intellectual pursuit, the Trinity always remains beyond the intellect's ability to comprehend. Even if we define the word person in terms of the Latin *persona* which means mask or face rather than a distinct personality, we have not simplified the complexity of the Godhead. The Father, Son and Holy Spirit are not merely alternate faces of God, but faces of persons that exist simultaneously in the one God. The fact that the Trinity is incomprehensible ought not to disturb us. If we could comprehend with our finite minds the nature of the infinite One, we could also wonder if such a deity had not been created by the comprehender.

For our purposes, it is more profitable to think of the person of the Trinity in terms of their functions rather than their distinctive natures. In any references to the Triune God it is the Holy Spirit who is most likely to be slighted. We do not quite know what to do with Him. It is more difficult to identify Him than the other persons of the Trinity. The very name Holy Spirit, or even worse, Holy Ghost, signifies the mysterious and intangible. When we refer to the Father, we have enough experience with fathers to get a tangible idea of the Heavenly Father. This is equally true of the word son which describes a familiar family relationship. Few of us would encounter any problem in conceiving of Jesus Christ who lived among us. But when we hear the words Holy Spirit, we face a vague sort of will of the wisp.

We experience this same difficulty when we consider the

functions of the Trinity. The Father is associated with creation and the story of creation immediately comes to mind. The Son is associated with redemption and His crucifixion comes to mind. But what can we associate the function of the Holy Spirit with—tongues of fire, doves, a babble of ecstatic sounds? The Holy Spirit is often identified as the Sanctifier, but this word is as mysterious as the term Holy.

In spite of this confusion, the fastest growing religious groups in America, the Pentecostal Churches, give special attention to the Holy Spirit. In addition to their emphasis upon the Holy Spirit, these Pentecostal churches emphasize religion as an experience. No matter how we may evaluate this movement, the association of the Holy Spirit with religious experience is defensible. The Son redeems the Father's creation and the Holy Spirit brings this redemption to the individual. He converts the facts of history into faith. He makes objective history become personal history—my history. He transforms "knowing about" into "knowing." He takes the good news of Christianity and makes it good news for me.

Of course this particular function is only an emphasis. God is One—therefore the Trinity is involved in all divine functions. The Son is also the Creator and the Father, Redeemer, even though the Father's function focuses in creation and the Son's in redemption. Thus, the Holy Spirit functions as the internalizer—the one who enables us to realize for ourselves the faith of our fathers.

Because of His function the Holy Spirit is defined in terms of the Church. He works within the fellowship of believers. It is through our relationships with people that God comes to us. We know Christ within the fellowship of those who believe in Him. Again, we can make an analogy with alcoholism. Alcoholics Anonymous reaches out to the alcoholic and brings him into its healing fellowship. In a similar way, the Church with the good news reaches out in love to those who need a Savior.

Since the Holy Spirit is associated with religious experience, the act of hitting bottom is in His domain. Indeed, we may say that He is dependent upon it, for it is the collapse of our ego defenses that opens the way to our spiritual growth. When we speak of hitting bottom, we are not implying that we pass this way just once. Growth is as continuous as the experiences related to it. Life pushes us in the direction of crises and the Holy Spirit uses the crisis situation to declare Christ unto us. He utilizes the natural to communicate the supernatural—the good news.

THE MESSAGE OF THE CROSS

When we give up the Holy Spirit takes over. When we surrender He receives us. He comes to us in the cross of Christ, and now the message of the cross makes sense: the cross is a picture of defeat. Moslems believe that Christ only passed into unconsciousness on the cross. They believe that for Him to die, especially in such a shameful way, would mean utter abasement and defeat. We recognize the value of defeat, however. In our crisis moments we are also in defeat, and the message of the cross speaks our language. God meets us where we are—at the bottom. Jesus' cry from the cross, "My God, My God, why hast thou forsaken me?" is the cry of One for whom all tangible hope has collapsed. God comes to us when all available resources collapse. He shares with us in this defeat. "God's acceptance of the cross," says Bonhoeffer, "is His judgment upon the successful man."[1]

---

[1] *Ethics* (New York: The Macmillan Company, 1954), p. 12.

It is God that qualifies rather than we. In Christ, He takes upon Himself our conflicts and suffers in them to the death. He identifies with us in our predicament, and triumphs over this predicament in His resurrection. In His triumph, we who are identified with Him, also triumph. The cross is our everlasting assurance that no sin can separate us from God, for "God was in Christ reconciling the world unto Himself" (II Cor. 5:19).

Here is a love demonstrated by sacrifice and suffering. By identifying Himself with our temptations and our sufferings, the Son of God became the Son of man. He comes to us where we are, even unto death—even unto death by crucifixion, that He might lead us to victory—to resurrection. The solution to our human dilemma lies in God's character rather than in our own—where, in our egocentric distortion, we are predisposed to seek it. This is what is meant by salvation by grace. This is what we mean by forgiveness through Christ.

FAITH AS THE ASSURANCE

How can a sign of defeat inspire confidence? The answer is simple: it inspires confidence because it was followed by a miraculous victory. Jesus speaks to us in our crises because He Himself was crucified. His identification in defeat and suffering would by itself, only create a bond of empathy. It would never give us hope. If the burial of Jesus in Joseph's tomb were the last episode in His career, His defeat would be no more a way of salvation than the death of Socrates some five centuries before. Socrates also gave his life for his principles, although in a far less humiliating and torturous way.

That which created the good news of Christianity was the

resurrection—the victory of Christ over the forces of evil
that had destroyed Him, even over death itself. In the words
of Charles Clayton Morrison: "The early Church grew from
eleven men to tens of thousands in that first generation after
Christ because it conquered death, the final enemy of every
living soul." But the victory came from no tangible source
for hope. The followers of Jesus were in despair when He
was crucified. They had no hope now that He was dead. To
believe in the mission of a dead Christ would mean to believe
despite overwhelming evidence of the contrary. For the
disciples of the Crucified, this was asking too much.

While they suffered in their hopelessness, God raised
Christ from the dead. Crucifixion now becomes the sign not
only of defeat, but also of victory. The incarnation is more
than a putting together of two substances, one human and
one divine. Rather, it is God's action in human life to
redeem that life—He acts in His way rather than in our way,
to save the world. As a sign of victory, the cross of Christ
inspires within the defeated the same hope for deliverance.
There is nothing in defeat itself to give hope. Hope comes
from without—from beyond the things that are seen. The
cross becomes a stimulus to faith because of the resurrection.

Kierkegaard said that the opposite of sin was not virtue
but faith.[2] He learned this from reading St. Paul. St. Paul
also said that the opposite of faith was sight: "We walk not
by sight but by faith" (II Cor. 5:7). Faith, then, is "the
evidence of things not seen" (Heb. 11:1). It is our assurance of progress in the face of concrete evidences of
failure. When we merely glance at the things that are seen,
we may see anything but progress. No wonder the ancient
Greeks failed to recognize any progress in history but saw
instead the futility of a cycle.

---

[2] *Sickness Unto Death,* p. 213.

The ancient Hebrews witnessed a similar futility in their own history. The Book of Judges can be called the book of cycles. It describes a time in Israel's history when every man did that which was right in his own eyes (Judges 17:6). This period lasted nearly three hundred years and was characterized by a cycle that repeated itself at least six times. The cycle started when the people began to ape the cultic practices of the Canaanites who inhabited the land. They "did what was evil in the sight of the Lord." Their degenerate acts aroused the anger of the Lord, and He gave them into the dominion of these neighboring peoples. In their anguish they cried out to the Lord for help—this is a kind of hitting bottom. Then the Lord sent them a judge or deliverer who drove out the oppressors and restored peace for a season. After the judge's death the cycle repeated itself.

Since the situation in Israel was no better after the sixth cycle than it was after the first, the futility is obvious. According to the evidence of sight, this was a meaningless epoch. When the Old Testament historian looked at things from the perspective of purpose, however, Israel's history was going somewhere and the period of the judges was part of this progress. The evidence of sight could not destroy this faith, for faith is not dependent upon sight. Nor did the historian have to deny the evidence of sight to establish his faith, for we do not have to run from reality in order to be hopeful. In times like those of the judges, we believe in God's progress in spite of what is happening rather than because of it.

Similar cycles are witnessed in our personal lives. Married people despair when their marriage seems to catch on a snag and the same old problems rise up repeatedly. Parents may grow discouraged when their children exhibit old patterns of immature behavior they supposedly had outgrown. People who work may reach a period when their line of progress begins to level off or take on circular pattern; they become discouraged by the same old routine and the same old difficulties.

Our own personality development often seems futile. We become frustrated over our lack of progress as we stumble back into old and hated ways of behaving. We fill up with despair over the mounting evidence that we are not getting anywhere—that our personality pattern is as fixed as the laws of the Medes and Persians. As François Mauriac said: "People do not change. At my age one can have no illusions on that point: but they do quite often turn back to what they were once and show again those very characteristics they have striven tirelessly, through a whole lifetime, to suppress."[3] We are like the traveler in the woods who believed he was heading in the right direction only to discover, again and again, that he was back where he had started—that he had been going in a circle.

CHRISTIAN VIEW OF HISTORY

What has the Christian good news to say to the meaninglessness of a circular existence? The good news is this: what may look like a circle is actually a line of progress to somewhere. "In the fullness of time God sent forth his Son, born of a woman, born under the law, to redeem those under the law" (Gal. 4:4). This fullness of time included both the apparent meaninglessness of the cyclical period of the judges, the captivity of Israel in Babylonia, and the contemporary conquest of Palestine by the Romans.

Is not all the above a matter of faith rather than of fact?

---

[3] *Women of the Pharisees*, (New York: Doubleday & Company, Inc., Image Books, 1959), p. 187.

The realist in our day wants to know the facts, but can we separate facts from faith in interpreting history? It is amazing how differently opposing factions will interpret the same "facts." In his book *Faith and History,* Reinhold Niebuhr concludes that historical facts are really *interpretations* of historical facts, and that the interpretation depends upon the point of view of the interpreter. Therefore, all interpretations of historical facts are matters of faith.[4] The Christian faith is a particular kind of faith. When it is applied to history, it says that God is at work to accomplish His own good ends regardless of how hopeless the situation may appear.

Does this sort of faith eliminate our responsibility for our own actions? No, not at all. Judgment is inseparable from God's good purposes. What this faith does eliminate is our egocentric need to *see* progress. We live in a success-minded age. We aspire to reach the top, to be influential, to ascend the ladder of progress. The desire for advancement can become the object of our distorted need to advance over others. Such distortion feeds upon sight rather than faith. Faith and egocentricity are incompatible. The ego can trust only itself. Therefore it must die so that the individual can have faith in God.

This faith comes into its own when the supports of sight are gone. In the face of the apparent meaninglessness of life, this faith can affirm itself in meaning. In spite of our obvious unworthiness, this faith enables us to believe in our justification—a justification *by* faith. In the face of something as final as death, this faith gives us the comfort of the resurrection. Because it is faith and not sight, it does not have to deny the negative to believe in the positive—to deny life to believe in God.

---

[4] (New York: Charles Scribner's Sons, 1949).

The "Simul" Principle

During the Reformation the good news was described by the words, "simul iustis et peccator"—which means "simultaneously justified and a sinner." This was the Gospel's answer to a guilt-ridden age. Guilt is real. We do not deny it to overcome it. Rather we affirm it, and in the face of that guilt, believe in forgiveness. The "simul" principle is that two opposites—justification and unworthiness—can exist together without denying each other. God justifies not the just but the sinner. This same principle applies also to death. We do not have to deny the reality of death to believe in eternal life. Resurrection means resurrection from the dead.

The most important application of the "simul" principle is to meaninglessness. It is here, says Tillich, that our age needs most desperately to hear the good news. If the Reformation period was characterized by the anxiety of guilt, then our age is characterized by the anxiety of meaninglessness. Too often we feel it necessary to deny this meaninglessness before we can believe in meaning. We do this by twisting things—by insisting on silver linings and devious half truths —so that we can show by sight that the universe is rational and all things are in order. We feel we have to demonstrate by sight that "all things work together for good to those who love God," before we can expect anybody—including ourselves—to believe it. In so doing we show our contempt for faith.

Now we are challenged to apply the principle of justification by faith to the anxiety of meaninglessness. We do not help God to forgive us by minimizing our sins—He does not forgive grey sins more easily than black sins. Neither do we help Him to resurrect the dead by carefully preserving the corpse in an airtight crypt. Nor do we assist the Almighty to put meaning into life by trying to show that meaning is already in life. Even as guilt is real and death is final, so meaninglessness is obvious. Yet in spite of meaninglessness, and not by eliminating it, we believe that life—our life—has meaning.

We find this "simul" principle of faith radically demonstrated in the Old Testament. When Elijah, the prophet, was afraid that the prophets of Baal would swing all Israel away from Jehovah, he challenged them to a contest to see whose God was the real God. Together they prepared an altar of animal sacrifice. Each was to call upon his God to ignite the sacrifice before the assembled people. When the prophets of Baal had failed, Elijah prepared to call upon his God. First he saturated the offerings with water—to make it crystal clear that God did not need to have things made easy for Him before He could act. Then he prayed aloud and the Lord answered with fire (I Kings 18:17-40).

God's ways are not our ways. We see this at the very beginning of His redemptive activity. He chose Mary, an insignificant peasant girl to be the mother of the long-awaited Christ. In her "Magnificat," Mary herself saw the reversal of the human value system. "My soul doth magnify the Lord," she said, "for He has regarded the low estate of His handmaiden . . . He has put down the mighty from their thrones and exalted those of low degree" (Luke 1:46:55).

Even in the Old Testament preparation for the redemption, we see this same operative principle. Abraham was told that through his descendants—the Hebrews—all of the nations of the earth would be blessed. To make this promise come true, Sarah, his wife, would bear a son. But Sarah's womb had been barren and she was beyond the age for conception. It seemed so ridiculous that Sarah laughed when she heard it. Nevertheless she conceived and bore Isaac.

The birth of the forerunner of Christ, John the Baptist, was very similar to Isaac's. Zacharias was also old and his wife, Elizabeth, was past the age of child-bearing. When Zacharias was informed by an angel in the temple that he and his wife were to become parents of the one who would prepare the way for Christ, he also doubted. As far as "sight" was concerned, it could not be done. Still, it happened.

It was not by human design that He who was born King was born in a barn, or that He grew up to be crucified as a dangerous criminal. He who from of old was described as the "mighty God" and the "everlasting Father," entered humanity as a helpless infant. He who is the "Prince of Peace," in His own words came not "to bring peace on earth but a sword" (Matt. 10:34). Although Lord and Master of all, He nevertheless washed His disciples' feet. He is true man and also true God. He is the sinless One, but He was made sin for us. His was the triumph of the resurrection, but it came out of the defeat of the cross.

THE CRUCIFIXION—RESURRECTION EXPERIENCE

Hitting bottom means the collapse of all the supports of sight, and therefore provides the opportunity for finding faith. In the Bible this experience is known as the crucifixion and resurrection experience. It is the means for progress because Christ identified Himself with it for redemption. Today, as we identify with Him in our own crucifixion experiences, we share in this redemption. He who cried out: "My God, my God, why hast thou forsaken me!" also said: "Father, into thy hands I commend my spirit." Here we see the affirmation of meaning in the very teeth of meaninglessness. Christ redeemed the experience of defeat by taking it to its ultimate end in death, and to its ultimate triumph in the resurrection. Now the triumph is ours because it was His.

Because of our human inertia, we are predisposed to stay on one level. To go higher would require the understanding that comes only from going lower. The insights that are inescapable in the crisis are often insights that were dimly perceived before. We needed a jolt to force them into the forefront of our attention. It is the jarring realities of crisis that open our eyes. Normally, our despair would prevent us from utilizing these insights, but the faith that we have in the resurrection makes this utilization possible. When by faith the Holy Spirit resurrects us again to a new realization of faith, we have the opportunity to put these insights into practice at the growing edge of our life. The deepest insights into ourselves and into our relationships may come in the most discouraging ways. It is to these regrettable moments that our spiritual growth is quite often indebted.

10
LIVING WITH MYSELF IN CHRIST

When I surrender to the God who comes in the collapse of my defenses, I no longer live with myself *alone* under *judgment;* I live with myself *in Christ* under *grace.* In the security of unconditional love we have no need for defenses: "If God be for us, who can be against us?" (Rom. 8:31) The cross says that God is for you! If God can accept us as we are, surely we can accept ourselves as we are. This does not mean that we condone our shortcomings or excuse our faults. To accept does not mean to excuse any more than to love means to admire.

Self-acceptance means that we can begin with the knowledge of what we are now, and continue on from that point. In other words, we can take ourselves where we are, in order to get where we want to be. This is what Kierkegaard described as movement at the spot as opposed to movement from the spot. Naturally we find it attractive to think of the desired as if it were the actual. When we allow ourselves to confuse the desired with the actual we then wallow in the despair of possibility—because everything is possible, nothing becomes actual.[1] This is movement from the spot—movement in imagination rather than in actuality. It will finally cease because only the spot is real—the spot of my present moment of existence.

An example of movement from the spot is the old time comic strip character, Major Hoople. The Major bored his boardinghouse cronies with tales of his great exploits. These exploits took place far from the living room from which the Major never seemed to depart. His actual situation stood in sharp contrast to the image in which he pictured himself. When his cronies confronted him with this contrast, he was irritated. Rather than accept the confrontation, he withdrew into fantasies of self-pity and retaliation. Because reality is painful, the task of changing it into the idealized is too difficult to attempt. Although Lady Macbeth was speaking of a bloodstain when she said: "Out, damned spot!" she expressed a universal abhorrence of movement at the spot.

When the necessity for judgment upon the present is eliminated, we can face reality with some degree of confidence. God removes this necessity when He receives us in our surrender. "There is now therefore no condemnation to those who are in Christ Jesus" (Rom. 8:1). If we are assured that there is no condemnation for those who are in Christ Jesus, then we can accept ourselves without developing a defensive ego image. When the press of judgment is removed, it becomes obvious that any self-acceptance based upon an illusionary picture of the self is a spurious acceptance. The good news liberates us from the compulsion to turn away from the spot. We learn the difference between

---

[1] *Sickness unto Death,* p. 169.

the illusionary self and our actual self, and we can accept this difference because there is no condemnation. When this happens we become "meek."

Perhaps no other word in the Bible is so completely misunderstood as this word *meek,* unless it is the word *humble* which means the same thing. The newspaper columnist Ann Landers used the word in its accepted sense when she identified it with the "shy violet. Although the Bible says that the meek shall inherit the earth," she wrote, "it's nice to have a little protection until the inheritance comes through." According to contemporary ideas, the beatitude could be interpreted as "blessed are the fainthearted." In a Biblical setting, however, the meek are those who have been liberated from the bondage of fear. If there are any who will not inherit the earth, they are the fainthearted!

The meek are not the opposite of the self-assertive, but of the arrogant—for they have nothing to defend. Our anger toward others is mostly projective. As one husband put it: "My wife brings out my own self-accusations (blast her!), and I attack her for this." But fear and hate are not the only reasons for attack: there is also concern for others. Jesus is described as meek when He rode into Jerusalem on Palm Sunday on an ass—the "lowly" king. That word could also be used to describe Him when He refused that same day to discourage the crowd from praising Him, and when He used physical force to drive the money-changers from the temple.

Because the meek can accept themselves, they have less need to be critical of others. They do not have to deny their own evil before they can believe in their own worth. As Noah said in *The Green Pastures,* "I an' very much, but I'se all I got."[2]

---

[2] Marc Connelly, *The Green Pastures* (New York: Holt, Rinehart & Winston, Inc., 1929), p. 68.

Moreover, because the meek have no illusions about them-selves, they can be honest. They alone shall inherit the earth because they alone can accept reality—even the reality of hitting bottom. Humility is inseparable from the crucifixion and resurrection experience: in the crucifixion experience we become humble because our ego defenses have collapsed; in the resurrection experience we become humble because we have been delivered. Our dominant sentiment is grati-tude—to be meek is to be grateful.

LOVE AS FORGIVENESS

We can see, at this point, how important our under-standing of God is for our understanding of ourselves. The experience of forgiveness takes away the need to escape. We can see also why forgiveness precedes repentance. Logically it would seem that forgiveness would come after repentance, for in repentance we express the desire for forgiveness. This is not the case, however, for in contrast to the hopelessness of despair, repentance is sorrow *with* hope. And that all-important hope springs from the good news, which changes despair into repentance by giving hope for acceptance.

When our mental image of God is something other than unconditional love, there is no good news. Usually the de-fensive ego-image takes its place. The pure and moral zealots, who hide behind a facade of righteousness as they denounce the wrongdoing of others, provide a good example of the defensive ego-image in action. I once counseled one of their number who described himself as a "fierce Christian." He was "zealous for the Lord," but in a hostile sort of way. His religion was all law and no love. The reason for this was clear: he had not received love. Like Tom Sawyer's Aunt Polly, he was "decent, regular and dismal."

The tension he created within others was a projection of the tension he harbored within himself. He was like Mauriac's Pharisee, "who spent her time dragging from room to room or wandering aimlessly around the table, strengthening her defenses against an attack that could come only from her."[3] Such is "the full horror of the torment that they inflict upon themselves, those servants of God who do not know the true nature of love."[4] He was in bondage to self-justification. When his bondage began to weaken, and he was unable to justify himself any longer, he descended into the hell of despair. He was redeemed from this spiritual bankruptcy by the good news of justification by faith. Now he did not need any fierce defense of his righteousness to block out his self-accusations; nor did he need to attack any outer evil to distract attention from his own.

We come now to the basic meaning of the word love. To love is to forgive. Jesus said: "Thou shalt love thy neighbor as thyself." Here is a formula for human relations that receives almost unanimous approval. The question is: how can we teach people to love themselves so that they can love their neighbor as themselves? This love for self which we so easily assume, is probably the most difficult of human accomplishments.

At the very mention of self-love we encounter misgivings. We figure that precisely what *is* wrong with people—they love themselves too much! "So long as I can remember," said a theological student, "I have been taught: 'be humble—do not be proud.' As a result I feel almost compelled to depreciate myself." Naturally with such self-effacement any idea of love for self would be repulsive. The only attitude toward self that could be tolerated by this distorted conception of righteousness would be self-rejection.

[3] *Op. cit.,* p. 168.
[4] *Ibid.,* p. 149.

Normally when we think of self-love, we think of self-praise rather than self-acceptance. Instead of thinking of *agape* love—love as forgiveness, we think of *eros* love—love of the virtuous, the excellent and the beautiful. Self-love is thus identified with self-conceit. If this were actually the case, we would have to change our whole understanding of the concept of love. A self-centered individual brings nothing but misery upon himself. He destroys his every opportunity for happiness by his selfishness. This is an odd way of showing love! Actually selfishness is a form of self-hate—of self-rejection. Anyone who must devote his energies to justifying himself, betrays his own sense of unworthiness.

When we grasp the idea of love for self in terms of God's love, the picture changes. Here is a love that centers in forgiveness. When I behold this love coming to me through the sacrifice and suffering of Christ, I am encouraged to extend this same love to myself. Then and only then can I extend it to my neighbor. We cannot give what we have not received. "We love because He first loved us" (I John 4:19). His love makes possible all other love. It provides the basis for a love that does not depend upon the quality of its object. How else could we love ourselves or our neighbor? And how can we love God as long as we are under His judgment? While it may be true that "to love another person means to see a miracle of beauty that is invisible to the rest of the world,"[5] it is equally true that love itself is the first miracle. It converts that which it loves into a miracle of beauty after it has first loved without the stimulus of beauty. *Agape* is always its own reason for being.

The three kinds of love support each other. Kierkegaard illustrates this mutual support by reversing the commandment: "You shall love yourself as you love your neighbor

---

[5] Mauriac, *op. cit.,* p. 107.

when you love your neighbor as yourself."[6] Love as forgiveness binds the three loves together. Visitors to Coventry Cathedral in England witness a tragic demonstration of this truth. Hitler's bombers needlessly attacked this beautiful house of worship until only a shell remained. This shell still stands as a monument to the horrors of war. It is a monument also to something that even war cannot destroy. Inside the ruins are engraved these words:

Father, forgive
All have sinned and come short of the glory of God.
The hatred which divides nation from nation, race from race, class from class,
Father, forgive.
The covetous desire of men and nations to possess what is not their own,
Father, forgive.
The greed which exploits the labors of men and lays waste the earth,
Father, forgive.
Our envy of the welfare and happiness of others,
Father, forgive.
Our indifference to the plight of the homeless and refugee,
Father, forgive.
The lust which uses for ignoble ends the bodies of men and women,
Father, forgive.
The pride which leads us to trust in ourselves and not in God,
Father, forgive.
Be kind one to another, tenderhearted, forgiving one another, as God in Christ forgave you.

---

[6] *Works of Love* (Princeton, N.J.: Princeton University Press, 1946), p. 19.

LOVE NEEDED FOR GROWTH

When I was a boy I was warned that smoking would stunt my growth. Although we still frown on children smoking, we no longer are so sure it will stunt their growth. Today, we believe a child's physical growth is determined by his heredity; his growth as a person, however, is not thus determined. This development requires love. If love is missing, the child will develop defensive illusions which will stunt his growth. Once blocked by these distortions, he can neither give nor receive love.

We most clearly see this happen in the development of the delinquent child. While it is never safe to generalize, there seems to be a sufficient trend among delinquent children to justify the following oversimplified description. The delinquent has often been so deprived of love that he has no self-image, not even an illusionary ego-image. Someone has to give himself to the child before the child can establish his own identity. When there is nobody willing to give, the child has so little identity that he becomes bored with the emptiness of his life. Richard McCann, an authority on delinquency, describes the good news for delinquents in terms of self-giving. Jesus, according to McCann, entered into this world of deprivation with "the gift of the self. As man He gave Himself totally to God. As God He gave Himself completely to man."[7]

Before the good news can be redemptive, it must bridge the gap between man and God, and man and his neighbor. The tie with God apart from our neighbor soon deteriorates

---

[7] *Delinquency: Sickness or Sin?* (New York: Harper & Row, Publishers, 1957), p. 109.

into a monologue with oneself. The tie with man apart from God soon exhausts itself in the futility of our mutual emptiness. In Christ we have both God and our neighbor. The tie with Him is a tie with God and man. Love for Him is love for God and our neighbor. His gesture on the cross creates a response from us that literally pulls us out of our egocentricity. He evokes from us gratitude and devotion by His own self-giving. His sacrifice was costly. We who receive its benefits are deeply involved in obligation. Since our response to His love goes beyond the man Jesus to the God whom He reveals, it climaxes in worship and praise.

It is this love of Christ that the Christian counselor seeks to convey. Christ's Spirit may be in our midst, but who can see a Spirit? We know about the intangible only through the tangible—thus God becomes a human being in Jesus Christ; thus Christ continues to be with us through His Church. He is still known through the gesture of self-giving. The counselor's techniques, therefore, are not important; it is the concern of one person for another that is important.

One of my students was trying very hard to help a hospital patient who managed to frustrate every attempt the counselor made to reach him. Finally the student counselor compassionately said, "Mr. Doe, I think you should face the fact that you are kidding yourself. You blame others for your troubles, and you change the subject whenever we begin to talk about your own responsibilities. If this continues you are going to spend the rest of your life in an institution. This is something I don't want to happen!"

The patient was taken aback. After a moment of silence he said, "You really care, don't you." This breakthrough initiated a change in the patient that eventually led to his discharge from the hospital.

In an economically depressed area where my students work with young people, one of the youngsters created a problem by his delinquent behavior. He was a tough little fellow of thirteen who had the characteristics of the delinquent child. After I had talked with him about the students' concern not only for the group but also for him, he became silent. I waited awhile and then said, "Will you do me a favor?"

"What is it?" he asked.

"Tell me what you are thinking," I said. "They're real swell guys," he said, and with that, a tear rolled down each of his freckled cheeks.

The realization that someone really cared for him will be a positive influence in this youngster's development. It may not be enough to overcome the deprivation he has known throughout his life, but it is a step—a wedge—in that direction. In his book, *Children Who Hate*,[8] Fritz Redl relates how he and his fellow workers lived with a small group of delinquent children for a year in an effort to supply them with the kind of relationship that they had been lacking. At the end of the experiment they found they had made little tangible progress. It takes wisdom as well as acceptance, and patience as well as wisdom to communicate love. There is no other way.

When we no longer fear ourselves we can learn to know ourselves better. We get to know ourselves in the same way we get to know another. We know another when we accept him as he is, and enjoy his company. Since we cannot tolerate others until we can tolerate ourselves, we can understand why knowing ourselves and knowing others go together— and why our love for our neighbor is patterned after our love for ourselves.

The fear of solitude, so common in our day, grows out of our fear of ourselves. Even those who keep to themselves

---

[8] (New York: Free Press of Glencoe, Inc., 1951).

may do so only as the lesser of two evils. Many of us run from the emptiness and boredom of our lives by drinking, by refusing to think, by making extra money or by buying some new thing. Money serves as a good distraction, and so do the things it can buy. They help us to be momentarily content with satisfactions that sooner or later will fail to satisfy us. We operate our radar station and stand ready to flee when anything resembling our inner conflicts is detected. We live on the surface. Fear shrinks our area of consciousness to a little island of trivialities—and these trivialities are temporarily distracted. When the processes of life begin to break down our checks and balances, we have our opportunity to repent. It is then that the love of Christ "casts out all fear," and provides us with a new orientation for living (I John 4:18). The good news restores us to our course. Now we can achieve a development as unlimited as the love that empowers it.

11
REMOVAL
OF
BARRIERS

Living with myself in Christ not only improves my relationship to myself, but also my relationships to others. "Only as far as a man is happily married to himself," said Novalis, "is he fit for married life."[1] What is true for the most intimate of relationships is true, to a lesser extent, for all relationships. The barriers to the self become the barriers to others. The barrier is defensiveness, and it is removed by the good news. We are made secure by our relationship with God, and therefore, do not rise or fall by what people think of us.

SECURE FOR LOVE

What will people think? How often have parents used these words to hold their children in line. This concern

---

[1] *Quoted in* Fosdick, *op. cit.,* p. 48.

about what others think is not eliminated by the good news. We are more interested than ever, because when we love someone, we are interested in him. What the good news does eliminate is the threat in what others think. It changes our reason for asking the question. My security depends upon something more than being respected by others. This fact alters my relationship to others: there is no reason now to be afraid of them. "The Lord is my helper"—here is my faith! Therefore "I will not fear what man can do to me" (Heb. 13:6).

When the question, "What will people think?" is a threat, the people in question are potential enemies. They can hurt us by judging us. For this reason many of our social groupings are composed of "friendly enemies." The conversation is pleasant and the faces are gay, but everyone keeps his guard up. The fear of exposure shows how little each trusts the other. The ancient vesper collect contains the petition, "defend us from the fear of our enemies," and not, "defend us from our enemies." The difference is important. It is fear that creates the majority of our enemies. Even those who may be our genuine enemies, derive their power over us through our fear of them. It is not from our enemies, but from the fear of our enemies that the good news delivers us. When we no longer fear them, we can love them. "There is no fear in love, but perfect love casts out fear" (I John 4:18). This is true even in relationship to God—for it is His love that casts out the fear.

Yet, the Proverb says that the fear of the Lord is the beginning of wisdom (Prov. 9:10). How then can love destroy that which is good? We have here another example of the complexity of language. The fear of the Lord which begets wisdom is an attitude of respect for the Deity. This kind of fear accompanies, rather than opposes, our love for God. God comes to us not to make us afraid of Him, but to identify Himself with us. The good news is not a business transaction with God, but a personal reunion with God. Consequently, we have no fear of exposure or of judgment, and love completes its work in the removal of the barriers. When we identify with God, we no longer fear the worst for it doesn't exist—the worst in reference to God is described as the day of judgment: "We know that love is perfected within us," says St. John, "that we have confidence for the day of judgment, because as He is, so are we in this world" (I John 4:17).

The more we are identified with God, the less we need our defenses with people. Ours is a security which cannot be threatened because it enables us to rise above natural attractions and repulsions. As human beings we are in bondage to a stimulus and response sequence. Given the stimulus, the response is sure to follow. The manipulators in our society operate upon this principle. This is the age of the "hidden persuaders," the "build-up boys" and the "Madison Avenue promoters," who show the same disrespect for the human personality as do the Communist brainwashers. Their success depends upon keeping their victims under the illusion that they are free even as they are being manipulated. Perhaps the manipulators may hold a cynical view of human behavior, but is it not the correct view? Otherwise, why are they so successful in obtaining results?

What these professional manipulators do to us on a mass scale, we also do to one another. I acted as counselor and teacher to a student who had considerable difficulty in releasing himself to do his best. His grades were far below his potential. Much to my delight he received an A on the first test he took after we had been counseling together. When I returned his test paper I said, "You did very well! Congratulations—keep up the good work." To my chagrin his next test was an F. "How come?" I asked.

"When I got that A," he said, "you complimented me. I knew you were trying to motivate me, and I wasn't going to let you do it."

The stimulus before us is similar to the stimulus of a waving flag, and our response depends upon the color of the flag. Red flags represent things that make us angry, and when these begin to wave we charge like bulls. They stimulate instant rage. The mere mention of the word predestination acted like a red flag on Lyman Beecher. Unlike many of the clergymen of his day, he believed that the predestination doctrine made God seem like a manipulator. On one occasion Beecher exchanged pulpits with a minister of this persuasion. When he arrived at the church the minister said, "Dr. Beecher, I wish to call to your attention that before the creation of the world God arranged for you to preach in my pulpit, and I in yours on this particular Sabbath."

"Is that so," said Beecher. "Then I won't do it!" He turned his horse around and went home.[2]

Did Dr. Beecher disprove predestination by this act or was it simply a reaction to a red flag? The resister is as bound to his need to resist as the conformist is to his need to conform. Thus neither our resistance, nor our compliance establishes our freedom of action.

There are other flags beside the red ones. There are black flags. These are the stimuli that fill us with fear, and when they wave we want to flee. But when flight is not possible, we experience the anxiety of the trapped. There are grey flags. These are the stimuli that discourage and depress us; when they wave, we feel worthless and defeated. Those who know us well enough to wave grey flags in our faces, can break our spirits. Finally there are white flags. When we see them unfurl, we become elated. Usually they convey some symbol of success that elevates our self-esteem.

---

[2] Fosdick, *op. cit.*, p. 15.

If we could be emancipated from this stimulus and response bondage, we could accept others when they lack a positive stimulus. *Agape* love can emancipate us, for it is the love beyond the stimulus and response mechanism of natural love. In the Greek language of the New Testament, *agape* love is the love of God, while natural love is called *philia* which is the love of friendship or *eros* which is the love for the beautiful or the noble. *Eros* love is a response to an erotic stimulus, even as *philia* is a response to a friendly stimulus. *Agape* love is its own stimulus. Therefore it frees us from the bondage to external stimuli. In the exercise of this *agape* love we live in the liberty of those who love their neighbor not only as themselves, but as Christ loves them. We can love our neighbor as he is.

When we are no longer afraid of people, we do not need to protect ourselves by withdrawing from them. Their rejection of us does not hold the threat over us that it once did. For we are anchored in God—and the stability of this tie allows us to risk involving ourselves with others. There is nothing as stable as unconditional love.

No Need to Withdraw

We experience a loss of face if our overtures to others are unsuccessful. This is because our security is based upon what people think of us. It is as if we had exposed our Achilles heel in a gesture of friendliness, and the other person had contemptuously rewarded us with a kick. The fear of such humiliation is enough to keep us from trying in any genuine way. When we withdraw in defense, we rationalize our withdrawal by professing indifference: "I couldn't care less!" or "To hell with him!"

This rationalization of indifference is only effective when our obligations go no further than our own self-interest.

When we believe in God, we are obligated to God. Faith is more than a support. It is a commitment, and as such, challenges our fear. Those who receive the good news are not only enabled to love, but are obligated to love. The words "thou shalt" are not removed by the good news; they are brought within the realm of possibility. Thus, thou shalt love thy neighbor not only as thyself but as Christ has loved you. Jesus, himself, enunciated this principle when He said, "Freely ye have received, freely give" (Matt. 10:8). The very reception of the good news draws us *toward* others.

I discovered the challenge of obligation in my first year in the ministry. There were people within my responsibility from whom I would naturally shy away. There was something about their personalities that was threatening to me. My reaction of withdrawal would be so automatic that I would normally have felt no need to justify it, but as a pastor, I could no longer do this. I was under obligation to God and to this person to move *toward* him. Once I recognized this, the person took on a new image in my mind. He was someone to get to know rather than someone to avoid. To my surprise I discovered that my overtures to these people were more often rewarded than rebuffed. Perhaps the fact that I was seeking more than my own interests when I made these efforts had something to do with their reception.

How many opportunities for involvement with others do we "write off" because of misgivings over our worth— opportunities which we may have explored were we obligated by love! Unfortunately, I needed a professional motivation to reckon with my obligations, but the obligation itself does not depend upon any professional status. The obligation I felt as a pastor differed only in degree, and not in kind, from the obligation that is ours by virtue of our orientation to God.

The fact that the obligation of love draws us toward people does not mean that we must always make the overtures. Our purpose is not merely the satisfaction that we have discharged our obligation—for this would be an egocentric distortion of duty. Our purpose is to succeed in our obligation of love. While love is directed toward a specific goal, its methods may be flexible. It also depends upon wisdom as the following anecdote illustrates. An effective church administrator once described how he dealt with some of the recalcitrant congregations in his district. "I have discovered that with some congregations as with some people, the wisest procedure is to give them a good letting alone. It seems to bring us together far better than constantly keeping at them."

His procedure was still an expression of his love. Sometimes when we are left to "stew," something begins to "brew." On the other hand, this method can also be used to retaliate —to "bring to time" those who have treated us disrespectfully. Our methods do not determine our motives, although our motives may influence our methods. Love needs wisdom to be effective, and wisdom without love leads to exploitation. One reason love never fails is that while it never gives up in its purpose, it is still free to alter its methods.

No Need to Please

In living with myself *in Christ* there is no pressure to lose my freedom—my individuality—in trying to please people. The good news makes it possible for me to give, without trying at the same time to get something in return. Several centuries before Christ, Aristotle taught that those who practiced the virtues of life were showing enlightened self-interest. This is the logic behind old saws such as: it is to our own advantage to cultivate ethical habits; even as crime does not pay, so honesty does; you can catch more flies with honey than with vinegar. In our day this sort of logic fits into the designs of the manipulators. An employer who is kind to his employees may get more work out of them. We cultivate good public relations when we are considerate of others' needs. In pleasing the right people, we are making a wise investment for future returns.

Dale Carnegie's *Little Golden Book of Rules* says that "giving honest sincere appreciation" is a "fundamental technique in handling people." A way to "make people like you" is to become "genuinely interested in them," and "make them feel important—and do it *sincerely.*" That such rules are given in apparent seriousness, indicates how little we are aware of what being sincere and being genuine really mean. When we separate the action from the motive, we change the nature of the action. What appears to be a gesture of kindness may actually be a wise technique. The debtors who had their debts reduced by the shrewd steward in the Bible story probably thought at the time that he was interested in their welfare. It was not long before they realized that his primary interest was in buying their good will. The good deal he gave them turned out to be an investment in his own future.

Most of us are not shrewd operators—we are simply frightened individuals. Our need to please is more instinctive than premeditated. We are attempting to disarm our would-be attackers by showing them how little they have to fear from us. But in our use of servile attachment, we are exploiting the virtue of kindness as much as the shrewd operator does in his aggressive manipulations. Our exploitation arises from our shaky confidence, however, rather than from any coldly calculated formulations.

In living with myself *in Christ* I am not so needy, for my needs have been met in the good news. Luther used the terms rich love and poor love to describe this difference. If our love is poor we have little to spare. We cannot afford to give any of it away unless we are reasonably sure of getting a return. There simply is not enough to go around. If, on the other hand, our love is rich, we can give without worrying about getting any back. We have enough to spare. Here is the security of the rich. They are released by their own abundance to concern themselves with others.

The love that meets our needs comes not only from the intangible witness of the Spirit of God, but also from the concrete expression of this witness in human fellowship. The realm of the spiritual takes place within the fellowship of human beings, and not apart from it. Fellowship with God apart from fellowship with people is too intangible to provide security. Christ is no more separated from His church than our spirits are separated from our bodies. In fact the Church is described as Christ's Body. He is the head and those who believe are members one of another in this Body. Our tie with Christ is as much in terms of our tie with other people, as the tie of the arm with the head is in terms of its tie with the other members of the body.

We may have to displease others for their own sakes. We may have to disagree with them simply because we care about them—say yes when they want us to say no, say no when they want us to say yes. We may displease them not only because we no longer fear them, but because we love them. Our disagreeableness simply makes us a more interesting personality. There is no one more monotonous and boring than a predictably agreeable person.

In counseling people who are coming to peace with themselves through the good news, there is an almost frightening sense of freedom in the air. Through the labor and travail of crisis, the self is coming to birth—or rather has broken its chains and is awaiting the courage to step out and be seen.

Old habit patterns, however, still block the way of the self's emergence. These people are still afraid—afraid to speak out—afraid they will be laughed at, misunderstood or criticized. This is an other-directed age of conformists, and everyone experiences this pressure to some extent.

At the same time, those who are experiencing the liberation of the good news are no longer content to submerge themselves in order to be safe. The counselor lends his support to their discontent. He helps them to see that they may have to risk a few enemies to have some real friends. There is small value in a relationship in which we cannot be free. The only way we can relate as equals is through honest communication. "Woe unto you," said Jesus, "when all men speak well of you" (Luke 6:26). Woe unto us—somewhere along the line we have probably sacrificed truth for tact and love for harmony.

Some of us adopt the conformist role as the only safe course for what we believe is our inadequate personality. A coed I counseled did this. She was convinced that she was worthless and unlovable, and that she had to be entirely compliant in order to make people accept her. She found a girl who needed to dominate and they became good friends. Counseling helped the good news to work its way in, and as the girl grew in her sense of self-worth, she became dissatisfied with her friendship. She saw with increasing clarity that it was a one-way affair in which she had little freedom of expression. On one occasion when her girl friend was belittling others, she gently confronted her with her own shortcomings. Startled by her unexpected boldness, the friend lashed out at her and then stomped out of the room. For several days their relationship was very cool, but in spite of this pressure the coed was able to maintain her new position of freedom.

After awhile the friendship was resumed, but it was now

on a deeper level. The girl friend understood without having to be told, that their relationship would have to be on the basis of equality. This story could have ended otherwise. The girl friend might have remained cool because she could not tolerate a friendship of equality. The coed had to recognize this possibility before she affirmed herself, or her girl friend's violent reaction would have pressured her into apologizing. She would have been brought to a renewed submission.

We, too, may have to risk a few blunders before venturing into the fresh air of self-assertion. If we must be absolutely sure that everything is going to be all right before we venture out, we will never make the venture. This is the place where faith enters—not faith that everything is going to be all right, but faith that even if we err in judgment or make people angry, God is still on the throne. It is through such a faith that this self of ours—created and redeemed by God —can come out and be seen.

It is important that our compulsion to comply be overcome through obligation rather than through rebellion. In rebelling we may be exhibiting only an egocentric desire to free ourselves from restraints. In affirming ourselves out of obligation, we are moved by loyalties that go beyond ourselves. Some of us may not be able to affirm ourselves until we become angry. The irritations must pile up until they reach a greater intensity than our fear. Anger is actually a reaction of fear. The defense is an offense. Sometimes we react by withdrawing or complying, and other times by attacking. In either instance we are defending ourselves against a threatening situation.

Perhaps you know the person who continually submits to abuse. He justifies his submission by saying he is turning the other cheek. But his motive is fear rather than love. The time may come, however, when the abuse becomes too much for him. In a tearful combination of humiliation and anger he may lash out at his tormentor. The reaction may be violent enough to make an impression and this may gain him a new sense of power. The next time he may explode under even less provocation. He has discovered that people are afraid of anger, and he may begin to exploit his new discovery by assuming a bullying role. He is no more reconciled to people than he was before, but now he has an aggressive rather than a submissive way of defending himself in a personal encounter.

Even as we may turn the other cheek out of fear rather than love, so we may refuse to turn the other cheek out of love rather than defiance. Love's course of action varies with its object. To turn the other cheek to some people may only increase their bullying tendencies. For their sakes we may have to resist them. Love is inner-directed rather than other-directed, for it centers in obligation. "With me it is a very small matter that I shall be judged by you or by any human court," said St. Paul. "I do not even judge myself...It is the Lord who judges me" (II Cor. 4:3). The most liberating of motives is "for Christ's sake."

No Need to Attack

In living with one's self *in Christ* there is no compulsion to get on top of others. We do not evaluate ourselves as persons by how we fare in relation to our competitors. This removal of self-evaluation from competition restores competition to its rightful place. Competition stimulates us to do our best. Since our value as persons does not rest upon getting to the top, we do not have to use competition as a defense. When we depend upon our competitive efforts to establish our worth, the efforts become too important—other values are pushed aside in the desperate attempt to excel.

We can see the influence of this defensive attitude toward

competition in the "win or else" philosophy of big time athletics. With the vocational security of the coach and the money of the speculators at stake, the players can no longer afford to be good sports. Too much depends upon the outcome. The unnecessary roughness in football and basketball may actually endanger the future of these sports. Thus our future as persons is also endangered by a ruthless attitude toward our competitive endeavors.

For the same defensive reasons some individuals are more comfortable in the underdog's position in competition. They cannot tolerate victory because it upsets their mental image of themselves. No one likes to lose, but some would rather lose than cause someone else to lose. They cannot tolerate the tension created by the loser's disappointment. They are afraid to hurt. To preserve their idea of a harmonious atmosphere, they unconsciously sabotage their own efforts. Sometimes they are even aware that they are holding back. But they remain at peace with themselves by not achieving more than they feel they deserve. By not crowding their opponents, they remain at peace with them and all the ties remain intact.

Contrary to the assumption of those who sabotage their own efforts in competition, we do not help others by holding ourselves back. The self-assertion of our neighbor does not depend upon our self-effacement. The compulsive loser is afraid to cause disappointment. Although he may assist his opponent to win, he does not help him to grow. The track star runs best when he has a good pacer. Even though he loses the race, he may improve his record because of the greater stimulation from a strong competitor. Of course, the competition can prove too much for us and we may simply give up, but then we are mismatched. In these instances we need a learning rather than a competitive type of situation.

Our value rests upon our Maker's evaluation of us. And

this is settled. When God's entrance into history in Jesus Christ becomes an entrance into our own personal history, we know God loves us. The feeling of unworthiness that we experience when we ask for forgiveness contrasts with the feeling of worth we experience when we receive forgiveness. Forgiveness elevates us to a new basis for self-evaluation. It places us into a relationship of unconditional love in which our worth as persons can be preserved. Here is our value, our dignity, our respect. God's vindication of us is the basis for our self-worth. Now we can "with confidence draw near to the throne of grace," and in this same confidence enter into life with people (Heb. 4:16).

The Christian life is a life of victory. "This is the victory that overcometh the world, even our faith" (I John 5:4). It is the victory of the resurrection. We see this victory most clearly in the conquest interpretation of Christ's atonement. In this interpretation of His redemptive work, Christ fought the battle with the enemy—the battle which began in the Garden of Eden. In the fall of man, evil is obviously the victor over good. But the struggle is not over. In His judgment upon the fall, God informed the serpent who tempted Eve that he would put enmity between its seed and the woman's seed. The result of this enmity would be that the seed of the woman shall crush the serpent's head while the seed of the serpent "shall bruise its heel" (Gen. 3:15). Christ as the one born of a woman, carried the battle with evil to its climax when he fought the tyrants who enslave and destroy the human spirit—sin, the devil, judgment, death. He took the full onslaught of all that the forces of evil could hurl against Him and when He died on the cross, evil had apparently triumphed. Evil's triumph was short-lived, however, for Christ rose from the dead. Good had actually triumphed over evil: "For as in Adam all die, so also in Christ shall all be made alive" (I Cor. 15:22).

12
THE JOY
IN
BELIEVING

When the Holy Spirit declares Christ to us, He brings joy to our hearts (John 16:22). This is because He brings us the *victorious* Christ. Thus in the resurrection there is joy, and this was the dominant note on that first Easter morning. Jesus' followers experienced the elation of victory as soon as their shock over His resurrection began to subside: "Then the disciples were glad when they saw the lord" (John 20:20). The joyous excitement of that first Easter returns in our Easter Sunday worship service. We thrill with Mary Magdalene as she realized that the man she thought was the cemetery caretaker was the Risen Lord Himself. "Master," she cried, and all her hopes were born again.

The resurrection was good news! The response is joy! At the close of his great chapter on the resurrection St. Paul exults, "Thanks be to God who gives us the victory through our Lord Jesus Christ" (I Cor. 15:57). "Rejoice in the Lord always; and again I say, Rejoice" (Phil 4:4). "Rejoice evermore" (I Thess. 5:16). Here we see the joy in believing.

Joy "in Spite of"

The joy in believing may be joy in spite of what is happening in the present moment. Many things occur in our day by day life that depress or elate us. The joy of believing grows out of a more stable stimulation than these irregular occurrences of elation. Moreover, the joy of believing can affirm itself in the absence of these elations. The rallying hymn of the Reformation centers upon this theme of joy in spite of present defeat:

> Take they then our life,
>   Goods, fame, child and wife;
> When they their worst have done,
>   They yet have nothing won:
> The kingdom ours remaineth.[1]

The joy of believing is an expression of the faith that overcomes the world. It does not have to distract itself from the negative issues of reality to affirm itself. Cyprian, a Christian martyr of the third century, expressed this joy in spite of evil to his friend Donatus:

> This seems a cheerful world, Donatus, when I view it from this fair garden, under the shadow of these vines. But if I climbed some great mountain and looked out over the wide lands, you know very well what I would see. Brigands on the high roads, pirates on the seas, in the amphitheatres men murdered to please the applauding crowds, under all roofs misery and selfishness. It is really a bad world, Donatus, an incredibly bad world. Yet in the midst of it I have

---

[1] Martin Luther, *A Mighty Fortress is Our God.*

found a quiet and holy people. They have discovered a joy which is a thousand times better than any pleasure of this sinful life. They are despised and persecuted, but they care not. They have overcome the world. These people, Donatus, are the Christians—and I am one of them.[2]

St. Cyprian contrasted the joy in believing with the pleasure of this sinful life, but he was talking about his own age. Paul Tillich draws the contrast for our day by differentiating joy from fun. "Of all the dangers that threaten our civilization, this is one of the most dangerous ones: the escape from one's emptiness through a 'fun' which makes joy impossible." Fun is "without passion, without risk and without love," a shallow, distracting, greedy way of seeking pleasure. It is often easier to unite joy with pain, he claims, than joy with fun.[3]

The prophet Habakkuk gives us a striking affirmation of joy in the face of loss. Speaking out of the value system of his rural society, he drew the contrast in the sharpest terms: "Though the fig tree do not blossom, nor fruit be on the vines, the produce of the olive fail and the fields yield no food, the flock be cut off from the fold and there be no herd in the stalls, yet I will rejoice in the Lord, I will joy in the God of my salvation" (Hab. 3:17). Pleasure and not joy is the opposite of pain. Both pain and pleasure depend upon the immediate stimulation of the senses. They are simple reactions that raise no questions beyond the immediate stimulus. The joy in believing has more stability because it confronts its contradictions as well as its supports.

The difference is comparable to the difference between

---

[2] *Quoted in* James A. Pike, *Beyond Anxiety*, (New York: Charles Scribner's Sons, 1953), p. 104.
[3] *The New Being*, p. 147.

the faith that overcomes the world and the naïve faith that Koestler attributes to communism. The Communist, he says, is characterized by his naïve faith in the infallibility of the Party, by his belief that the end justifies the means and by his contempt for the bourgeois ideals of sentiment and morality.

Rubashov, the tough old Communist boss, had never raised any questions about his faith. Then, as a prisoner awaiting trial in his own Party prison, he began to wonder about the correctness of his position. "Must one pay for deeds which were right and necessary?" he asked himself, questioning whether the end can really justify the means. A dryness came into his throat and pressure arose against his forehead as he continued to seek answers. "Was there another measure besides that of reason? . . . Was his debt perhaps, counted double—for others knew not what they did? . . . What is this— a breath of religious madness?" For the first time since his arrest Rubashov was frightened.[4]

Unlike Rubashov's faith, the faith that overcomes the world has faced its doubt. The joy that arises out of this faith has its opposite not in pain but in sorrow. Sorrow results from our confrontation with the evils in life—with the irrational order of things. The joy in believing includes sorrow because it is joy in spite of sorrow. It can go beyond sorrow without denying sorrow, because it is the joy of the resurrection. The concentration is on overcoming. The focal point in the vision ahead is victory, and the resurrection of Christ supplies a foretaste of that victory. We see this emphasis in the invincibleness of Jesus' own trust as He commended His spirit into God's hands while He despaired. This acceptance of evil is not a stoic resignation to the inevitable; it is a positive confrontation with evil made pos-

---

[4] Koestler, *Darkness at Noon*, p. 56.

sible by our confidence in God. We commit ourselves
—and our problems—into His hands, not as an escape from
our own responsibilities, but as the only way of penetrating
problems which at the moment seem insuperable.

It was said of the early Calvinists that they feared God
so much that they feared nothing else. Our problems are
not that we fear—only a fool could live our kind of existence
without fear. Rather our problem is that we fear the wrong
things. It is not necessary to eliminate fear, but we must
learn to fear the right things if we want to develop. The
fear of the right thing is a positive fear. It draws us out of
ourselves to a higher loyalty and devotion.

Joy of Personal Fulfillment

The joy in believing is the joy of personal fulfillment.
"Thou hast created us for Thyself," said St. Augustine, "and
our souls are restless until they find their rest in Thee."[5]
God has created us in His own image so that we might have
fellowship with Him. The fall of man is the fall from God's
image. This means it is also the fall from God's fellowship.
In his fallen condition man is something less than human.
He is unsatisfied because he is incomplete. He is like a
married person without his spouse. Once two have become
one, they are incomplete when separated. "As the hart
panteth after the waterbrook, so panteth my soul after Thee,
O God" (Ps. 42:1). Thus the psalmist pictures the void
in the soul estranged from God. As a deer thirsts for
water after his chase, so the human being thirsts for God in
the midst of all his activities. By ourselves we have only
our own salty tears which aggravate rather than quench

---

[5] St. Augustine, *Confessions*, I, 1.

thirst: "My tears have been my food day and night" (Ps. 42:2). We need a vertical as well as a horizontal fellowship to satisfy our human desires.

The joy in believing is the positive vitality that comes from having received the vision. The emptiness that characterizes our age is created by the loss of that vision. We need the vision in order to have identity—the meaning for which I search has to be a meaning for *me*. The vision provides us with the creative fulfillment that comes from being called. The call is often associated with the call to the ministry. Many dramatic stories surround the call, and students of theology are frequently concerned about whether or not they have experienced it. But the call is to more than the ministry. It is the call that comes to each recipient of the good news; it shows him how to contribute himself to God's purposes.

Our sense of identity comes from our sense of purpose. Our need is to give as well as to receive. Says Tillich: "People are sick not only because they have not received love, but also because they are not allowed to give love."[6] I shall never forget the plaintive lament of a mental hospital patient when he said, "I have no one who needs my love."

The vision provides us with the vibrant hope that comes from being a somebody. Kierkegaard spoke of the individual in his day as being "ground smooth as a pebble" by society —of being "a cipher in the crowd."[7] If this was true a hundred years ago, how much more is it true in day of mass population and mass production. We run from the row houses of the slums to the identical bungalows of the suburbs. In striving to become the same as everyone else, we end up as nonentities. And this is the basis for our

---

[6] Tillich, *op. cit.*, p. 48.
[7] *Sickness unto Death*, p. 167.

emptiness and subsequent despair. There is no identity in sameness; identity grows out of our uniqueness.

Those who differ from us in national or racial characteristics look alike to us. As the Chinese grandfather said in *Flower Drum Song*, "All white people look alike." But of course all Chinese people look different from one another. Other people's children also are hard to differentiate. They all seem to be alike. But how different each of our own children is from the others! When we think of people in terms of their sameness, we treat them accordingly. By ignoring their individuality we show them disrespect.

The uniqueness of each person is symbolized by his name. His name belongs to him alone just as do his fingerprints. "A man's name is to him the sweetest and most important sound in any language"[8] because it focuses on his uniqueness. The fear of being a nobody haunts us all. It is this fear that is overcome in the good news by the personal touch of knowing the One who knows us by name. "But now thus says the Lord, He who created you, O Jacob, He who formed you, O Israel? 'Fear not, for I have redeemed you; I have called you by name, you are mine'" (Isa. 43:1).

The vision in which we are called by name satisfies our need for importance. Most of us have been irritated at one time or another by someone's obnoxious sense of self-importance. Its very obnoxiousness indicates that this self-importance is a compensation. It is overdone because it is covering over the opposite—a deep and unwanted fear of being a nobody—a nothing. When our sense of importance is genuine it does not have to be emphasized. It comes to us from the One to whom we belong and to whom we are obligated.

---

[8] Carnegie, *The Little Golden Book of Rules.*

Joy of Positive Action

The joy in believing is the joy of positive action. The note of victory in our faith gives us confidence, and confidence leads to action. Without confidence we are immobilized by our inhibitions. There is no frustration more severe than that created by the desire to do on the one hand, and the fear of trying on the other. The personal stalemate that these opposing forces bring about is as painful as it is pathetic. The hope of victory counteracts this fear of trying, and the joy that follows is the joy of doing.

A young lady who experienced the frustration we have described, disciplined herself to settle for safety. She was able to so control her appearance that she gave the impression of apathetic indifference. Behind this façade she concealed a very frightened person who had an intense desire to please. She didn't want to recognize her fear-ridden self —nor was it easy for her to allow herself to see the vision that she coveted. In order to preserve her facade she had to stop her efforts to develop herself. Since there is no joy in inactivity even if there is safety, she wound up in a chronic depression that finally led her to seek counseling.

Her progress was painfully slow because of her facade. Gradually she was able to admit to her creative desires. She gained the courage to tell me that she thought at times that God had destined her for some important task. Between these inner dreams and her outer efforts there was a great gulf, a gulf with which she found it increasingly hard to live. She began to despise her defensive self-curtailment, but could she accept the obligation to try? The old fears returned, but faith had also taken hold. She made the effort with some degree of success, and this boosted her confidence.

It even gave her the courage to accept an offer of marriage although she still possessed too little self-confidence to believe that she could succeed in marriage. She had matured enough to realize that her choice was either inactivity with depression or effort with fear. Her actual reward was different. She learned the good feeling in accomplishment—the joy of positive action.

St. Paul said, "I can do all things through Him who strengthens me." By itself, his statement is nonsensical. Surely, I have limitations to my abilities that even faith in Christ cannot overcome. Within the relationship of faith, however, this affirmation is easily understood. It applies to those areas in my life where I have been inhibited by fear and inferiority from developing my fullest potential.

The positive action that creates joy is action at the spot. Those whose joy is the joy in believing are able to face reality because their belief has encompassed reality. Their belief also obligates them to Another. When we are obligated only to ourselves, we can manipulate these obligations to fit the circumstances. We can hardly take such obligations seriously. But, when we are obligated to Another, the obligations are unalterable. To take them lightly to is become insincere.

Kierkegaard warned against this tampering with what it means to be earnest in the story of the two gamblers. Both believed that they should quit gambling, but for different reasons. The first gambler said, "I promise by all that is high and holy that I shall never more have anything to do with gambling, never. This evening will be the last time." This man, says Kierkegaard, is not serious. His movement is from the spot and not at the spot. He will never quit.

The other gambler said to himself, "Now, then, you may gamble every blessed day the rest of your life, but this evening you shall leave it alone." Here is movement at the spot. He will quit. He will know the joy of positive action. Self-affirmation brings joy because through it our creative nature finds expression.[9]

JOY OF ENJOYMENT

The joy in believing is the joy of enjoyment. Enjoyment is something we are not always sure we should have. When it remains unchallenged for too long a time, it threatens to upset the precarious balance we have achieved and thus destroys our peace of mind. This happened to a certain salesman. Whenever he felt good about things, he had the uneasy fear that this feeling could not last. The more he fought this feeling the stronger it became. As he himself put it: "It seems that part of me is bringing up things to worry about, and another part is fighting against thinking about these things." He was fighting against himself and therefore could only lose. When he struggled he simply increased the conflict.

After he had fretted away enough time for his sales to drop, he seemed to recover his old balance. His equilibrium was maintained by a relentless balance of credits and debits which precluded any real enjoyment of life. Enjoyment—such as that which he received from his work when his sales were high—pushed him too far into the debit column. The tension this created caused him to sabotage his enjoyment by stirring up a worry. Although this made him miserable, it also enabled him to move into the credit column. When his sales situation became critical, his worries shifted to this external problem, and he was able to throw himself into his work again.

---

[9] Kierkegaard, *For Self-Examination* (Minneapolis: Augsburg Publishing House, 1940), p. 53.

The good news encourages us to put our whip on the shelf. The cross makes it unnecessary to inflict punishment upon ourselves. The good news is that we have been released from this compulsion to punish ourselves by God's own identification with our punishment. The victory of Christ becomes our victory. The good news redeems us from the bondage of the law of just deserts to the freedom of grace. Grace means that our joy needs no self-imposed limitations to keep things in balance, because forgiveness maintains this balance. The fact that our covenant with God is a covenant of grace means that it is *gratis*. The question of deserving it does not enter the picture.

The victory of Christ takes us into life, for it is life that is redeemed. The love that we receive from God directs us outward. The joy in believing is the joy of fellowship with believers. The dominant characteristic of the early believers that we read about in the Bible was their joy in each other's company. The good news had created a community:

> And all who believed were together and had all things in common; and they sold their possessions and goods and distributed them to all, as any had need. And day by day, attending the temple together and breaking bread in their homes, they partook of food with glad and generous hearts, praising God and having favor with all the people. And the Lord added to their number day by day those who were being saved (Acts 2:44-47).

The good news means that the whole of life is sacramental. When we think of sacraments we think primarily of Baptism and the Lord's Supper. In these rites established by Christ, He chose elements of our common life to communicate the blessings of His redemptive activity. In Baptism we use water to convey the covenant relationship with

God that Christ has effected for us. In the Lord's Supper
we use the staff of life and the fruit of the vine to convey the
elements of His sacrificial love—His body and His blood. By
using elements of this created world to convey the blessings
of redemption, the sacraments proclaim the good news that
redemption has restored this created world to its rightful
place. He has given us the things of this world to enjoy.
"For everything created by God is good and nothing is to be
rejected if it is received with thanksgiving; for then it is
consecrated by the Word of God and prayer" (I Tim. 4:4).

The sacramental principle extends from the sacraments
into life as a whole. This world of nature, people, things and
events is sacred because Christ participated in it to overcome the forces of evil. Now it is restored to its original role
as a means through which we acknowledge and receive the
Creator. He wants us to enjoy the good life that He has given
us. And when we do, He wants us to respond with thanksgiving. One of the earliest names for the Lord's Supper was
"the Eucharist," which means "the thanksgiving." Thus in a
broader sense our enjoyment of God's creation can make of
our life a Eucharist:

> Behold what I have seen to be good and to be fitting
> is to eat and drink and find enjoyment in all the toil
> with which one toils under the sun the few days of his
> life which God has given him, for this is his lot.
> Every man also to whom God has given wealth and
> possessions and power to enjoy them, and to accept
> his lot and find enjoyment in his toil—this is the gift
> of God. For he will not much remember the days of
> his life because God keeps him occupied with joy in
> his heart (Eccl. 5:18-20).

"This is my Father's world," says the children's hymn.
It is our Father's world not because of any sentimental at-

titude over the goodness of the world; not because we can see how everything works together in an intelligent and beneficial way. It is our Father's world only because it is redeemed. Even the evil must ultimately serve His purposes. The faith that overcomes the world is the belief that in the midst of our involvement in life "all things are working together for good to those who love God, to those who are called according to his purpose" (Rom. 8:28). Here is the joy in believing.

13
ON TO VICTORY

Throughout the previous chapters we have discussed the predicament in which we human beings find ourselves, the goods news as the answer to this predicament and the way in which the good news is realized. The way in which this goods news is realized, however, is not something that happens to us just once. Actually it occurs again and again, for the way of realizing the good news is also the way we grow as persons.

WAY OF BEGINNING IS THE WAY OF CONTINUING

Pastoral counseling students often ask whether there should not be a difference between counseling people who have known the good news and those who have not. My answer is no. In the first place it is difficult for anyone to make such a discrimination. In the second place there would be no difference in counseling procedure because the approach that helps people to receive the Christian faith also helps them to grow in their faith. The good news is realized anew in each crisis. The way of entering into God's grace is also the way of growing in this grace. The experience of justification by faith is not only a beginning experience but a repeated experience.

The repetition of the justification experience meant for Kierkegaard that faith is a turbulent thing. To illustrate this he imagined that Luther had returned from his grave to talk with him.

"Are you a believer? Do you have faith?" asked Luther.

Kierkegaard answered, "As all others call themselves Christians and believers, I also will say, 'Yes, I am a Christian.'"

"How then," asked Luther, "have I not noticed something about you, and yet I have observed your life—and you know faith is a turbulent thing. To what end have you been disturbed by the faith you say you have?"

Kierkegaard replied, "Yes, but dear Luther, I can assure you I have faith."

"Assure, assure—what kind of talk is that?" said Luther. "As far as faith is concerned, no assurance is needed if one has it (for faith is a turbulent thing and is noticed immediately), and no assurance can help if one does not have it."

"Yes, but just the same believe me!" Kierkegaard protested. "I can assure you most solemnly—"

"Ah, stop your talking! What good can your assurances do!" Luther interrupted.

"Yes, but if you would only read one of my books you would see how I present faith; so I know I must have it," said Kierkegaard.

"I believe the man is crazy!" said Luther. "If it is true that you can present faith, it merely proves that you are a poet, and if you do it well, that you are a good poet—anything but that you are a believer. Perhaps you can also weep when you present faith; it would merely prove that you are a good actor." True faith—like real love—is a restless thing as it inwardly deepens us.[1]

Faith is a turbulent thing because it is characterized by crucifixions and resurrection experiences. These experiences occur over and again in the believer's life. We cannot initiate the crucifixion and resurrection experience, but we can run from it. When we do, we stunt our growth. Those who receive the good news are those who have the courage to ask the question: what is God attempting to show me, to say to me, now—in all that this "now" contains? Instead of "leaning upon our own understanding," we "acknowledge him in all our ways." Only in this way can he "direct our paths" (Prov. 3:5-6).

Since there is no condemnation to those in Christ Jesus, we can look into the present moment without fear of being condemned by what we see. With the anxiety of condemnation diminished, the need to escape is also diminished. Through the disturbance of crucifixion and resurrection, the Holy Spirit shapes us into the image of Christ. As a purging process, the crucifixion experience opens our minds to a deeper understanding of our needs and shortcomings. The resurrection experience is the leap in faith by which God restores us to confidence and hope.

If the way up is down, we may not be aware of our own growth. Instead we may be aware only of our need for growth. How could it be otherwise if humility is at the center of growth? In spite of our lack of awareness, we can continue to believe we are growing. We need not depend upon the evidences of sight for this belief, for we have the evidence of faith—"the evidence of things not

---

[1] *For Self-Examination,* pp. 12-13.

seen" (Heb. 11:1). We believe that in spite of the evidence of sight, the recurrent crucifixion experiences are not simply cycles of defeat, but are essential paths to our growth.

St. Paul expressed this belief when he said, "But one thing I do, forgetting what lies behind and striving forward to what lies ahead, I press on toward the goal for the prize of the upward call of God in Christ Jesus" (Phil. 3:13-14). The good news helps us to forget the past when it discourages us or makes us complacent. It helps us to remember the past when we can learn from it. The mark of a maturing person is the ability to profit from past experience. Our lapses provide us with the understanding that is needed to press on to victory.

There are times, however, when our growth is obvious, and we know that we have changed. These are precarious moments. Will our reaction be gratitude or pride? Will we think that God has succeeded with us or that we have succeeded for God? Our egocentric distortions may sabotage our growth at these precise points. When this happens the relationship with God that has been established by the good news is also sabotaged. Despite the repeated crucifixion of our ego by the Holy Spirit, we continue to harbor within us both the distorted and the undistorted—a tension which St. Paul described as the conflict between the flesh and the Spirit (Gal. 5:17).

The flesh, which is our egocentric distortion, is rarely victorious when it openly defies the Spirit. More often it succeeds by clouding the issues in such a manner that it appears to be allied with the Spirit. Thus it steals the Spirit's victories. In our success we may assume that God must surely be proud of us. This is the pride that goes before the fall. The flesh reduces our sense of dependency when it subtly "takes over," and in overestimating our own sufficiency, we set ourselves up for a fall.

Further enlightenment may come only through failure.

We may have to lose a battle to win a war. Complacency, on the other hand, comes easy. As creatures of habit we tend to solidify rather than to grow. In one way this is good, for our habit patterns provide us with stability. In another way it is dangerous because we may cease to question our habits and that can be deadening. We become less like persons and more like machines. Only when some genuine spontaneity on our part breaks into this mechanical consistency, are our personalities restored.

When our supports collapse, complacency ceases and spontaneity takes over. Out of this fresh, albeit negative experience, the Holy Spirit resurrects us to a new vitality. We rise again from the death of the old—not to solidify on any new level of understanding, but rather to die again. Here is the dynamic movement of growth—of life. The rise to a higher level of development is preceded by a retrogression in which a fresh encounter with reality takes place.

A Courageous Approach to Life

The good news that frees us from the tyranny of fear also gives us the courage to go forward. With the removal of threats, we are more likely to involve or commit ourselves. The good news has taken away the terror of crucifixion. We neither seek it nor avoid it. Here again, however, the flesh may sabotage the Spirit by appearing to join forces with it. Thus when a person seeks crucifixion for the purpose of self-punishment, he destroys the meaning of the crucifixion experience. It is no longer a valid crucifixion, for crucifixion is genuine only when there is no tangible benefit in sight—humanly speaking it is a totally negative experience. Thus when the flesh perverts the crucifixion experience into a way of self-punishment, it is up to its old trick of usurping God's place.

The ego can trust no one—especially God. It prefers the tangible evidence of punishment to any ego-deflating promise of forgiveness. However, the ego is afraid to trust this punishment to another, and therefore seeks to inflict it upon itself. Again, we see how every victory of the flesh undermines the good news. The experience designed to cause the ego to die can be distorted into the means for keeping it alive.

When the fear of failure is strong enough to deplete our courage, we believe the way the timid servant did in Jesus' parable. This is the story: A master called in his three servants prior to his departure, and gave one five talents, another two talents and another one talent, each according to his ability. On his return the master demanded an accounting. The servant who had received five talents had invested these and had five more to show. The one who had received two talents had an additional two to show. However the servant who had only the one talent had buried it in the ground, and therefore could only present the original talent. In his defense he said that because he knew that his master was a hard man, he was afraid to invest what little he had for fear of losing it. The master condemned the servant with his own words. You knew I was a hard man—therefore you should have invested my money with the bankers. When we are obligated to produce, there is really no safety in withdrawal. So take the talent from him, and give it to him who has the ten talents. What we do not develop, we finally lose (Matt. 25:14-23).

When the people of Israel entered the promised land they were charged to drive out all the Canaanites who were living there. This was a cruel charge according to our contemporary humanitarian viewpoint. These people had lived in the land for centuries. They, too, were human beings. From the viewpoint of Israel's calling, however, the charge was the lesser of two evils. The Canaanites were a degenerate people. If they remained in the land they would be a continuous temptation to the Israelites to deviate from their divine calling. Toleration of the little opens the door to the big. The Israelites, however, stopped short of total victory. As soon as they had achieved a measure of success, they slackened their efforts and became interested in side issues. When the situation was no longer urgent, they grew careless as well as fat and prosperous.

The seeds of destruction were already planted within their borders. They had been warned that these remaining Canaanites would become as "pricks in your eyes and thorns in your side" (Num. 33:55). But the Israelites had lost sight of their commitment. The people began to indulge themselves in the immoralities of the Canaanites. As they grew soft, these Canaanites rose up and conquered them. These, then, were the oppressions in the cycle of the Judges to which we have referred.

The challenge is before us. The goal is victory. We, too, are obligated to drive out the Canaanites. And like the Israelites we also tend to grant ourselves a little license after we have had a measure of success. This indulgence shows that we too resist complete victory. When the external pressures are relieved, we have nothing from within to keep us at the task. Commitment alone can supply this. Our attitude is an indication of whether we are using God or God is using us. In their oppression the Israelites cried out to God to drive out the Canaanites. Once the oppression ceased, they felt little obligation to press on to complete victory.

The danger comes after the initial success. With nothing from without to press us forward, we allow ourselves to be lulled into indifference by a false sense of security. Only our commitment can move us then—only an obligation that is based on faith rather than sight. Carelessness in victory may lead to tragic defeat. Alan Guttmacher remarks that "Getting a little bit careless about birth control often results in getting a little bit pregnant."[2] His facetious observation has a wider application: a careless attitude is already destructive because it is a betrayal—a sell-out—of our commitment.

Behind any supposed desire for perfection there is also a fear of it. We need a few vices, we say, to keep us humble. We fear we can't take it. Others say that they need a few vices to keep human. They are afraid their neighbors cannot take it. Should we become perfect, we would upset our whole adjustment.

The fear that follows victory is the fear that there are no more worlds to conquer. It is of course an illusion, and subsequent crucifixions dispel it. The fact that we experience it, however, shows that we have an unconscious resistance to push onto total victory—to drive out all the Canaanites from the promised land. We have a fear of altering our self-image. That *status quo* offers us security. Even though we are dissatisfied with it, we fear to push very far beyond it. This is the fear of the unknown. As Charlie Carmody said in Edwin O'Conner's *The Edge of Sadness,* "I'd a damn sight rather stay here. Where I know what's what." If we pushed on to perfection there would be nothing to feel guilty about—and there is security in guilt. It tells us "what's what."

It is ironic that complete redemption is foreign to our desires, since complete redemption is the hope of heaven. Jesus said, "Be ye perfect, even as your Father in heaven is perfect" (Matt. 5:48). But is perfection really attractive? The common attitude toward it would lead us to the

---

[2] Alan Guttmacher, *The Complete Book of Birth Control,* (New York: Ballantine Books, 1961), p. 83.

negative answer. An individual who is perfect would be dull if not naïve—more of a stick than a person. Most of us prefer sinners in preference to such saints. Surely they are closer to the kingdom of God.

When we look at Jesus we do not see a colorless or passive person. He called King Herod a fox and denounced the Pharisees as hypocrites and blind guides. Certainly these were not nice things to say. It was He who made a whip of cords and drove out the money-changers from the temple and then poured out their coins and overturned their tables. Surely this was much too violent an action for a saint. Jesus' perfection was not a congenial passivity; it was a complete devotion to the calling of God. For this cause—His cause—we dare to press on to perfection.

Like the Israelites we tend to drift into peaceful coexistence with the enemy when there is no immediate threat. Not only do we settle for something less than completion —which may be simply an acceptance of reality—but we cease to be concerned about completion. What we accept in the present and what we have in mind for the future ought always to be different. If our goals are too low, our development deteriorates. On the other hand if we cannot adapt to reality, our high goals only serve to frustrate us. Here, too, our development deteriorates.

All progress is relative to the final goal of perfection. Our full development is a goal which is always in tension with our present development. The good news converts the contrast between what we are and what we are committed to become, from a frustration into an inspiration. Growth becomes possible when we can accept our imperfection without giving up the goal of perfection. When either one of these is omitted, growth becomes stymied.

If we are unable to live with our imperfection we must

either repress what we cannot tolerate or torture ourselves with recriminations for our shortcomings. This is the dilemma of the perfectionist. He feels so basically unacceptable that only perfection can give him a sense of worth. On the other hand if we become so well adjusted to our imperfection that we no longer are sensitive to any commitment toward perfection, we develop a complacency that is stultifying. This is the dilemma of cheap grace. There is no obligation to our acceptance—therefore there are no goals to our life. We are simply drifting.

Final Victory Assured

The joy of the resurrection experience grows out of the awareness that the final victory is assured. It is the joy of the Easter discovery that the great negatives of life —the defeats and destructions that climax in death—are only temporary. "Because I live," says Christ, "you shall live also" (John 14:19).

The assurance of final victory means that we have hope of eternal life. This hope is not simply a hope for survival. There is a difference between a belief in immortality and the good news of eternal life. A part of most cultures and of most religions, the belief in immortality, is the hope for the survival of death. Few of us like the idea of dying. Something about life seems to indicate that it cannot end. Death is a tragedy, and we do not accept it gracefully. Our natural tendency to want to survive is so strong that we think that a person who commits suicide must be mentally unsound. His action is abnormal—even pathological.

There are people who act as though they were never going to die. There are people who refuse even to think

about death, particularly their own. But death is too universal to give even our wildest fantasies any hope for
thinking we can escape it. Our only recourse is to hope
for a survival of death.

While the hope for eternal life has something in common
with our natural desire for survival, it is quite different in
most respects. The hope for mere survival is transcended
by the resurrection hope for the final victory of good over
evil. It is the victory expressed in the Hallelujah Chorus
of Handel's *Messiah,* where the kingdoms of this world are
triumphantly proclaimed to be the kingdoms of our Lord,
and of his Christ; and he shall reign for ever and ever.
"For he must reign until he has put all his enemies under
his feet. The last enemy to be destroyed is death" (I Cor.
15:25-26).

Not only shall the victory of Christ be fully realized, but
—and here is the good news for me—I shall participate
in this victory. Christ's triumph over the powers of evil
shall include my own triumph over my own evil. "Then
shall I take hold of that for which Christ once took hold
of me" (Phil. 3:12). Here then is the goal of redemption:
that I shall be enabled to love the Lord my God with all
my heart and to love my neighbor as myself. This is the
Christian understanding of perfection—the fulfillment of
the law in love. It is a perfection that begins within and
works out—a perfection that begins with the motive.
When our redemption is complete we shall be restored
to the Divine Image even as we respond completely to the
love of God. All biblical descriptions of the eternal life give
centrality to God's presence. In the eternal fulfillment, our
communion with Him shall be without distortion and
without interruption. This will restore us to our full
humanity.

The hope of eternal life is an otherworldly hope. In

contrast to otherworldly escapisms, it throws us into a worldly involvement. The expectation of the future that expects victory has already conquered the future. The believer is, therefore, reconciled with the future as he functions in the present. That which is settled no longer has power to disturb. The anticipated victory gives us confidence for our present involvements.

If the future hope were not connected with the present moment, it could easily degenerate into an escapist dream. Redemption in the future is a completion of the redemption that is going on now. Belief in eternal life in the midst of death is the big leap of faith—all other leaps are practice jumps. The *now* already has the eternal dimension within it; it is all part of the same piece. Our hope in God for the future is inseparable from our involvement with God for the present. This is why defeat in the present is not really defeating. The worst that it can be is a temporary setback— a setback as temporary as the Crucifixion of Christ. The purpose of the cross was realized largely in retrospect. So the meaning of our defeats is not confined to a this-worldly perspective. We perceive also within the perspective of faith. No wonder Jesus said, "Blessed are the eyes that see the things that you see." (Luke 10:23).

The hope of eternal life gives us an advantage over the Communists in the use of thermonuclear weapons. Only the most insufferable boor speaks glibly about atomic warfare, and the worst of these is the religious boor who says, "Let it come—heaven is my home." Such an unthinking, unfeeling type of piety is an offense to the compassion of Christ. It is an otherworldly superficiality which lacks any sense of corporate guilt, honest confrontation or Christian responsibility.

In spite of our abhorrence of even the thought of nuclear war, the fact remains that the Christian has no continuing

city here. We seek rather the city yet to come (Heb. 13:14).
If civilization is destroyed by a nuclear holocaust the Communist dream is over because the Communist lasting city
is here. The Christian dream is not. For although the
Christian dream relates itself to the here and now, it has
an eternal dimension that is not confined to the here and
now, and therefore cannot be destroyed by atomic bombs.
"We are God's children now; it does not yet appear what
we shall be, but we know that when He appears we shall
be like Him, for we shall see Him as He is" (I John 3:2).
To see Him as He is means that we shall be like Him, for
only then shall we see without distortion. "And every one
who thus hopes in Him purifies himself as He is pure"
(I John 3:3).

> Though the cause of evil prosper,
> 　　Yet 'tis truth alone is strong;
> Though her portion be the scaffold
> 　　And upon the throne be wrong,
> Yet that scaffold sways the future,
> 　　And, behind the dim unknown,
> Standeth God within the shadow,
> 　　Keeping watch above his own.[3]

---

[3] James Russell Lowell, "Once to Every Man and Nation." *Service Book and Hymnal*, (Minneapolis: Augsburg Publishing House, 1958).